LEADING FROM THE SECOND CHAIR

How to lead without a leadership position

by

Dr. Abraham Manase

Copyright Information

Dr. Abraham Manase
Website: www.drmanase.com
E-Mail: Abraham@drmanase.com
Leading from the Second Chair: How to lead without a leadership position.

Copyright@2021 by Dr. Abraham Manase
ISBN: 978-1-7369389-0-4
Copyediting: Karen Simmering
Cover Design: Ariana Knox

Printed in the United States of America

LEADING FROM THE SECOND CHAIR

How to lead without a leadership position

Dedication

This book is dedicated to my parents, my late father Jonasi Manase and my mother Margaret Mphephu "N'waMhelembe" Manase, who have always encouraged me to study. My father used to say, "A pen is mightier than a sword." ....He was right!

Recommendations

PRAGMATIC! "Dealing with things sensibly and realistically in a way that is based on practical rather than theoretical considerations." That is the first word that came to my mind when I read "*Leading from the Second Chair.*" Because, when considering the indispensable subject of leadership and leadership teams as this book does, pragmatism is precisely what we need.

If this book is nothing else (and, most assuredly, it is much more), it deals with the easily practical counsel. The guidance found in this book is born of Dr. Manase's comprehensive personal experience of serving in positions of elegated authority and many examples of others in "second chair" leadership positions and delegated responsibilities. I highly recommend this book as required reading for any leadership team.

- Dr. Prince Maurice Parker
Professor of Theology-Assemblies of God Theological
Seminary, La Carlota, Córdoba, Spain

Shalom, Jesus is the owner of the church; He always says, "Come unto me, and learn from me." He is therefore leading from the first chair. He appointed some to be apostles, prophets, evangelists, teachers, and pastors to equip Christians for the work of ministry. Looking at Christ as our first chair, we all occupy and lead from the second chair. The one on the first chair is the Rock, on whom the entire church is built. This book, *Leading from the Second Chair*, will help and guide our leaders from all spheres of life to understand that leading is not a position, but a function and responsibility. You do not have to be elected to be a leader.

Thank you, Dr. Manase, for unearthing such a hidden treasure in you. We praise the Lord for His wonderful works and for using you to change so many lives throughout the world. I recommend that everyone who is in any form of leadership or serving in any capacity read this book. Once you read it, you will never see or understand your position the same way you did before.
Bless you.

-Dr. Bishop Moses N Shipalana

Apostolic Faith Mission, Fountain of Life Church, South Africa

I recommend the book, *Leading from the Second Chair*, especially because I know the author very well. Dr. Abraham Manase is my friend, and he writes from his personal experience. For those of you who don't know him, I want to let you know that even though he is someone who is highly accomplished in life, in ministry, and academically, he is always serving with excellence. The first time I met him in America, he was serving his pastor and my team with humility and excellence. I will use this book to train and develop our leadership in Brazil and other countries that I will visit. There is a lot of wisdom in this book, Obrigado.

-Pastor Daniel Procopio
Igreja Internacional Novo Dia, São Paulo, Brazil

I have known Dr. Manase for more than three decades. I have personally known him since high school as a brother in Christ and a schoolmate. From his formative years as a youth, Dr. Manase has always been an influential leader. He had great influence in the church, the local community, and the Student Christian Movement (SCM). He is a remarkable, trustworthy leader, a faithful brother, and a dear friend to me. He is a humble man with a servant leader's heart and always influential like yeast in dough.

In this gem, *Leading from the Second Chair*, Dr. Manase touches on the vital aspects of serving as an assistant under the main leader. In most cases, you never hear about the people who lead from the second chair, until they are appointed as the main leaders. Dr. Manase addresses significant issues that if they are not taken care of, could impede the very inception, progress, and development of leadership. He keeps on emphasizing that leadership is different from a position. He delicately and thoroughly discusses leadership as a calling, rather than a mere title.

I guarantee you, God is about to change your destiny as you read this book. I highly recommend this book to all who are serious about taking their leadership skills to the next level, whether in the marketplace or in ministry. This book has been released for such a time as this to affect, influence, install, and bring about change in the life of every reader,
In His service,

-Pastor Sifiso Hendrick Chauke
Kingdom Faith Church Ministries, Milton, Keynes United Kingdom

Thank you, Dr. Abraham Manase, for blessing the world with such a valuable piece of life-changing work. By the grace of God I have been serving in leadership roles for the past 35 years. I served as a second chair leader for 15 years and as a first chair leader for 20 years. I would love to appreciate Dr. Manase for this unique powerful leadership tool.

One of the reasons there is so much frustration and premature ascension to first chair leadership is the lack of knowledge and appreciation for the second chair leadership. Unfortunately, this usually results in the abortion of great destinies. I would love to highly recommend this book to all leaders, both first and second chair leaders. This book will help us to play our role as leaders in harmony without strife and unnecessary conflicts. This is more than just a book; I see it as a valuable leadership training manual. The book also addresses the issues of succession plans in leadership, a subject that is rarely touched. Once again thank you, Dr. Manase, for empowering every leader with this leadership manual.

Thank you.

-Pastor Strike Manganyi
General Overseer of Manna Tabernacle Family Churches,
South Africa

Leading from the Second Chair is an authentic manual for 21st-century leadership. In this book, Dr. Abraham Manase brings revelation knowledge on how each of us can actually create impact from whatever level or position we are in our organization with or without any title. His approach to leadership solves the most common crises in church organizational leadership, in fact in any organization. *Leading from the Second Chair* provides the much-needed strategy for raising strong leaders and empowering them to serve at their full potential while recognizing the unique challenges of serving in a subordinate position. Last but not least, this book equips leaders with the attitude, skills, and knowledge in a practical way to improve the performance of their organizations. This is a must-read for anyone in leadership!!!"

In His Kingdom

-Dr. Mishael Carson
Missions to the Balkans, Poland.

Foreword

In October 2009, I sat alone on a bench overlooking a grove of mango trees in Tzaneen, South Africa. I was the leader of a team of 26 short-term missionaries, and we had just concluded our ministry work and were preparing to return to the United States. I was pondering the launch of New Day Christian Fellowship in Corona, California, which was to take place in a few weeks. I had never considered being a senior pastor. I had been very comfortable supporting my senior pastor, but God had other plans for me.

Abraham Manase, originally of South Africa but now an American citizen informed me that he and his family would be charter members of this new church venture. Neither of us knew for certain what lay ahead, but we were trusting that God was with us. Indeed, He was, and the church launch was successful.

While the attendance of our local church increased incrementally over the years, what surprised us all was the significant impact of our international outreach. By October 2019, our network included 22 churches in North and South America, Asia, and various African nations.

During the course of this time, Abraham Manase was ordained as a church Elder at New Day. Not only does he oversee various ministries in our local church, but he has also provided a great deal of doctrinal and leadership training to thousands of church leaders in other nations.

I have witnessed first-hand Elder Manase's great ability at leading an organization from a secondary position. He manages the internal tension between contentment and progression quite well. My pastoral peers continually remark to me, "I need an Abraham!"

Elder Manase also excelled in his career, where he has received numerous promotions. He places a premium on education and professional development. He received his earned doctoral degree in business administration. I mention this because even with the demands of family, his busy career, and educational endeavors, Dr. Manase faithfully adds value to the New Day Global Network of churches.

I am very passionate about Jesus' question to us in Luke 16:12, "And if ye have not been faithful in that which is another man's, who shall give you that which is your own?" Is it possible you have not received our own because you have not served faithfully in that which is another man's?

Leading from the Second Chair will aid you well. Read slowly. Take copious notes. Ponder as you go. May the eyes of your understanding be enlightened (Ephesians 1:18).

Blessings,

-Bishop Tony Dunn
New Day Global Network

Introduction

I have always been fascinated by seeing some organizations do well; however, some do not succeed in the same environment and market. The same applies to churches: There are some churches that thrive, and there are some that struggle. One main contributing factor in determining the success of any organization is leadership. As John Maxwell always says, "Everything rises and falls with leadership." People's understanding of the concept of leadership makes a big difference in any church or organization.

Concepts and their interpretation are crucial. We all behave and respond to situations based on our understanding of the concepts. The concept of leadership is often misunderstood. Many people associate leadership with position, so they wait and do nothing, expecting the so-called "leadership" to do something about their situation. I have seen a lot of infighting among leadership in organizations, ministries, and churches. People fight for positions because they are convinced that the only way one could lead, serve, or make a difference is when he has a position. Everyone can make a difference in the church; nobody should undermine himself. If you think you are insignificant, it means you have never slept with a mosquito in your room.

Most leadership books focus on the senior leader in the organization like the senior pastor, company CEO, and school principal. A few books focus on the assistant or their supporting staff.

This book focuses more on anyone who is serving under someone's leadership like an assistant pastor, vice-chairperson, assistant administrator, deputy director, church elder, deacon, or anyone playing a supportive role. In my many years of leadership experience and my international travels, as I interact with leaders globally, I have noticed that there are a lot of people who struggle with being in second chair or assistant positions.

In this book I would like to bring a different angle and view of leadership. I will focus on how you can lead and make a positive difference even when you do not have a position. Yes, you can lead without a position. We will notice that there is a difference between leadership and position. Brighten the corner where you are.

TABLE OF CONTENTS

Acknowledgments..ii

Chapter 1:   Successful Leadership............................1

Chapter 2:   Second Chair Leadership........................8

Chapter 3:   Timothy..10

Chapter 4:   Joseph...21

Chapter 5:   Aaron..27

Chapter 6:   Elisha...33

Chapter 7:   John Mark..41

Chapter 8:   Understand the Limits of Your Authority....55

Chapter 9:   Submission.......................................62

Chapter 10: Move from Dependency to
              Interdependency 68

Chapter 11: Teamwork Makes the Team Work............71

Chapter 12: Manage the Contentment-Dreaming
              Tension...78

Chapter 13: Leave a Legacy...................................81

Chapter 14: See Your Senior Leader as a Gift from God..86

Chapter 15: How to Leave Your Church....................90

Chapter 16: Pray for your Leaders and their Families......96

Chapter 17: Focus on Making Your Pastor's Vision a
Reality..99

Chapter 18: Be a Source of Encouragement and Appreciate
Your Leader..................................101

Chapter 19: God Loves FAT People Be Faithful, Available
and Teachable...............................104

Chapter 20: Keep a Positive Spirit.........................112

Chapter 21: Communicate with Your Pastor..............115

Chapter 22: Receive Admonitions with Grace............118

Chapter 23: Be an Exemplary Leader.....................121

Chapter 24: How to Increase Your Value in Your
Organization.................................123

Conclusion...135

Notes...136

Author..138

ACKNOWLEDGEMENTS

Firstly, and foremost, praise and thanks to God Almighty for the strength and help that He gave me to complete the writing of this book.

I cannot express enough thanks to the love of my life, my supportive and loving wife Mihloti Manase. Thank you so much for always believing in me and trusting that I can do more and better even when I did not. I would also like to express my deepest gratitude to my children (Nsovo, Timothy, and Hope) for their great support, patience, and encouragement. If it were not for their support, this book would not have been realized. They were patient with me for countless hours and sleepless nights that I spent in the office working on researching and meeting the project deadlines.

Bishop Tony Dunn has always been a source of inspiration to me. God crossed our paths for a purpose greater than we could imagine. He has always been with us through our challenging and difficult moments. *Leading from the second chair* came as a result of him giving me an opportunity to research more on this obscure subject, and always offered me a chance to practice these principles under his leadership at New Day Christian Fellowship.

I cannot forget my best friends, pastors Thomas and Sonti Mbungana; and pastors Aubrey and Constance Shikwambana. We have been friends since boyhood, we grew up together, we became family friends and did a lot of ministry work together both locally and internationally, their encouragement and confidence in me has always been tremendous.

There are so many pastors that I served under for the past 30 years, including Bishop Moses Shipalana, pastor Adolph

Machimana, and Bishop Ed Smith. They made me who I am today by giving me an opportunity to serve under their leadership.

A special thanks goes to all of you who took your time to read my manuscript, especially my editor, Karen Simmering, who was always thorough and on time.

PART A
Chapter 1
Successful Leadership

Work willingly at whatever you do, as though you were working for the Lord rather than for people. (Colossians 3:23 NLT)

John Maxwell defines leadership as simply influence. To have influence means to have an effect on the condition, or to affect or alter by indirect or intangible means. Influence is not cohesion but the capacity of a person to produce effects on the actions, behavior, and opinions of others. People voluntarily follow an effective leader because they believe that their lives will change. When you are a good leader, people will not follow you by manipulation, force, position or cohesion, but will follow you voluntarily because you have a positive impact on their lives. Leadership is not a position, but influence. People volunteer to follow their leaders, not their positions. When you have leadership skills, people do notice it and will follow you. I have been to a school where one teacher had more influence on the staff and the students than the principal. The principal had a position or title, whereas the teacher was the leader.

Transformational leaders help people reach their goals. Once a person discovers that you are genuinely interested in his growth, he will become loyal to you as his leader. Leaders build trust based on how they treat people. You cannot lead people without a foundation of trust. If people do not trust you, they will make it difficult for you to lead them. You cannot successfully lead people who are suspicious of you. If you have a challenge in leading your people, check the level of trust in that organization or structure. Some essential leadership skills and practices that could help build trust are self-development, team development, innovation, strategic thinking, and acting ethically.

Transformational leadership is the approach that causes a change in individuals and social systems. Transformational leaders create valuable and positive change in the followers with the end goal of developing followers into leaders. Transformational leadership focuses on individualized consideration, intellectual stimulation, inspirational motivation, and idealized influence.

Successful leaders convert a crisis into an opportunity.

Captain Chesley Burnett "Sully" Sullenberger is an American retired Air Force fighter pilot and airline captain. He is best known for his role as a pilot in command in the 2009 ditching of US Airways Flight 1549 in the Hudson River off Manhattan, NY after both engines were disabled by a bird strike; all 155 people aboard survived. Now he is a speaker on aviation safety and has helped develop new protocols for airline safety. Before this incident, Captain Sully was just a pilot like any other pilot. It took one incident to reveal his leadership skills and expertise. When your organization is going through a crisis, instead of being an ordinary employee, resident, or member, emerge as a leader who brings in solutions to the situation. Do not cry, complain and blame—make use of the crisis to show up as a leader.

The Chinese word for "crisis" is pinyin; the same Chinese characters for pinyin are used for "danger" and "opportunity." When there is a crisis, ask yourself how you can use it as an opportunity. It is all about mindset and perspective. I am not referring to using people's pain to manipulate them and benefit yourself from their misery. You could use the opportunity for mutual benefit. In actual fact, a business is only successful if it meets the needs of the community that it serves. I always advise people about two main principles in business: Firstly, never get into a business if you do not understand how it works. There are a lot of people who make a fortune through stock market investments; however, I also know a lot of people who joined the stock market without understanding how it works and lost all their investments. If it does not make sense to you, do not risk your money until you understand what you are putting your hard-earned money into.

The second piece of advice is to make sure that your business serves what the current community needs. I lived in Southern California for more than 20 years, and I have seen some cities and communities that went through a demographic transformation. Some grocery stores thrived as the Hispanic population grew. These are the businesses that evolved with the demographic changes; when they noticed the increase in the Hispanic population, they evolved and started selling more Hispanic food. I lived in Anaheim next to Disneyland for many years, and I observed that supermarkets like Albertsons started to close their doors. The reason these stores were closing is because the leadership resisted the new realities; they did not want to change and start selling Hispanic groceries. The same thing happened with companies like Blockbuster, who used to rent out VHS cassette movies. They refused to change to the digital era and were forced to close because the world converted to digital. Now people watch movies on Netflix, Hulu, Amazon Prime, YouTube TV, and others. Nobody goes to the store to rent a movie anymore. As a leader, do not become irrelevant like Albertsons and Blockbuster.

Every person who comes under your leadership has a need, and as a transformational leader, you have an opportunity to help them meet that need. When you meet people's needs, you become a successful leader. People always follow a leader who focuses on helping them grow. They follow a leader who shows genuine interest in their growth and development.

I have noticed that true, strong, and genuine leaders usually emerge when there is a crisis because they always focus on finding solutions for people's crises, needs, or problems. Sometimes you do not have to solve their problem, but you can give them advice or at most an ear. In most cases, people just need to be heard. Situations, crises, and problems create or reveal true leadership. God will always bring situations that create opportunities for you to lead. When you see a crisis situation in your church, community, organization, look at it as an opportunity for you to lead the organization toward a solution, no matter what your position is. Pray and ask God to give you the wisdom to lead.

Be a problem solver leader

The bigger the problems that you solve, the more value you add to the organization. If you want to be recognized as a valuable member of the board, committee, organization, or church, identify areas that the organization has challenges on and bring a solution to the area. If the organization has serious challenges with managing its finances, you may train to be the best accountant and help improve the organization with financial management. In case they have to lay people off, you will be the last one to leave the company because they see value in you.

Remember, the bigger the problems you solve, the more you will get paid. Under normal circumstances, people who earn bigger salaries are the people who bring solutions to society's bigger challenges. People's priorities matter; they are willing to pay as much as they can as long it helps solve their problems. That is the reason according to *Forbes* the following industries are said to be the richest industries today: financial services, technology, healthcare, real estate and construction, communication, food, manufacturing, education, renewable energy, entertainment, and fashion and retail.

Your value in the organization is based on your contribution to its success. Generally, people who solve big problems are the ones who are paid more. People respect you more when you bring solutions to their situations, not when you bring more problems to them. Next time you approach your pastor, supervisor, or manager, give them an explanation of the current situation and the problem, then before you finish, suggest a few possible solutions. Do not sit across the desk and stare at them and expect them to bring a solution to your crisis. All managers love people who bring solutions to them; it makes their lives easier.

Successful organizations and leaders are not afraid to hire people who are better than them. When you are an assistant to your leader, don't be an assistant by title; you must become that dedicated valuable assistant. When you are a good leader, results will show. As they always say, numbers do not lie, good leadership results in the success of the organization. Everything rises and falls with the leadership. I have a principle that I call the "rule of 80." Eighty percent of problems in any organization are caused by poor leadership, and 80 percent of the solutions come from the right leadership. In actual fact, when people leave the organization, church, company, or any institution, in most cases they are not leaving the organization, but their leaders, managers, or supervisors.

Being a great visionary leader

Great leaders can lead without a position—there is a lot that you could do without a position. You could focus on solving problems, bringing solutions to a situation, and give direction when people do not know what to do. Sometimes people just need someone to pray with them during a crisis—that is great spiritual leadership right there. You do not need to be voted into a position to pray with someone.

Great leaders have a vision. They are able to see what others may not see. Vision may not necessarily mean sight, but the ability to see beyond now. Vision is the function of the heart, whereas sight is the function of the eye. Leaders have an ideal church, family, or organization that they want to build. The organization may not exist yet, but they could share with you what they see happening in the future. They could give you the square inches or square meters of what they want to build. Vision is the blueprint of any organization. Great leaders are pregnant with a vision. Great leaders who have seen it before it happened are confident and have strong convictions like Martin Luther King and Nelson Mandela. When you have the vision, and you have seen where you are going, nobody can talk you out of it. Leaders have a strong conviction. If you don't give people a vision, they will come up with their own. It's hard to serve when the vision is not clear.

PART B
Chapter 2
Second Chair Leadership
What is a second chair leader?

A second chair leader is someone in a subordinate role whose influence with others adds value throughout the church or organization. It is important to understand that ultimately, in Christ's Kingdom, no matter your position of service in your organization, church, community, or government, we are all in the second chair because we all submit to Christ as the head of the Church. Second chair leaders lead even when they are not the top leaders of the organization. They have influence even without a position. They focus on serving and helping people. True leadership focuses on making other people's lives better and helps them grow. Great leaders leave their organization in better shape than it was when they came in. They leave the organization in a better financial, spiritual, and stronger position than they found it. Great leaders make an impact in the organizations and lives of the people they lead. People should feel better or in a much better position emotionally than they were before they met you. The most important thing that second chair leaders focus on is making an impact. One can be a great leader without a position.

Second chair leaders in the Bible

The Bible is full of leaders who did a great job as second chair leaders and assistant leaders. We will look at the following five examples: Timothy, Joseph, Aaron, Elisha, and John Mark.

Chapter 3
Timothy

You have heard me teach things that have been confirmed by many reliable witnesses. Now teach these truths to other trustworthy people who will be able to pass them on to others. (2 Timothy 2:2 NLT)

Timothy appears in the New Testament as Paul's most trusted assistant. Timothy was probably born in Lystra, the son of a Jewish mother, Eunice, and a gentile Greek father. Little is known about his father, and no evidence is ever given regarding his Christianity. Possibly, it was Paul who filled the shoes of a spiritual father to Timothy. Scriptures show that Eunice converted and became a Christian (Acts 16:1; 2 Timothy 1:5). Timothy was about sixteen years old when he and his mother were converted to Christianity. The name of Eunice's mother (Timothy's grandmother) was Lois, and she too became a Christian, possibly during Paul's first evangelistic journey to the city in Acts 14.

Paul knew three generations of this family. He knew Timothy's grandmother Lois, his mother Eunice, and Timothy himself. Paul believed so much in the value of three generations, he emphasized it when he gave Timothy the final instructions. He instructed Timothy to teach what he had learned to faithful men, who would, in turn, teach others.

The New Testament depicts the relationship that existed between Paul and Timothy's family for over 20 years. As a leader, you have to take time to know your disciples, team members, mentees, and successors in ministry. Do your best to know and understand their families as individuals. Paul understood that Timothy was a person who came from a family, and he honored that. This made it easy for Paul to advise the churches that Timothy would visit and tell them how they should treat Timothy when he came.

Jesus also emphasized the importance of knowing the person that you are mentoring. "My sheep listen to my voice; I know them, and they follow me." (John 10:27 NLT) You have to show personal interest in people as a good leader; do not treat people as a group but as individuals. People are not tools but human beings with feelings and emotions. Be considerate when you deal with them.

Paul had a very close bond with Timothy; he would usually address him as "my son Timothy." (1 Corinthians 4:17; 1 Timothy 1:18; 2 Timothy 1:2) Paul considered Timothy a true son in the faith because he probably led him, his mother, and his grandmother to faith in Jesus on his first missionary journey. "5 I remember your genuine faith, for you share the faith that first filled your grandmother Lois and your mother, Eunice. And I know that same faith continues strong in you. 6 This is why I remind you to fan into flames the spiritual gift God gave you when I laid my hands on you." (2 Timothy 1:5, 6 NTL)

Timothy joined Paul and Silas on their second missionary journey and traveled with them over modern-day Turkey. When Timothy was about 21 years old, Paul picked him up on his second missionary journey (Acts 16:1). Timothy served closely under Paul's ministry for the rest of his life. Paul invested a lot of time, attention, and energy in training him. He traveled extensively with Timothy, deliberately training him and exposing him to intense ministry experience. Paul left Timothy with the church at Ephesus so that Timothy might help them. It was while he was serving this church that he received the two epistles (letters) which bear his name, the 1st and 2nd Timothy in the Bible.

Paul also gradually introduced Timothy to all the churches that he had established. In most of his letters, Paul made sure that these churches knew about Timothy. Paul trained Timothy to do everything that he had learned over the years in ministry. For a long time, I thought Paul trained Timothy to be a good preacher of the gospel only; however, the more I studied the Bible, the more I discovered that he trained him in many areas. Paul trained Timothy to be great as an assistant writer, servant leader, missionary, messenger, teacher, preacher, and evangelist. Paul knew that Timothy would need all these skills to be successful in ministry. The following scriptures reflect on what Paul trained Timothy to do.

Assistant writer—Timothy assisted Paul in writing six books of the Bible

This letter is from Paul, chosen by the will of God to be an apostle of Christ Jesus, and from our brother Timothy. I am writing to God's church in Corinth and to all of his holy people throughout Greece. (2 Corinthians 1:1 NLT)

This letter is from Paul and Timothy, slaves of Christ Jesus. I am writing to all of God's holy people in Philippi who belong to Christ Jesus, including the church leaders and deacons. (Philippians 1:1 NLT)

This letter is from Paul, chosen by the will of God to be an apostle of Christ Jesus, and from our brother Timothy. (Colossians 1:1 NLT)

This letter is from Paul, Silas, and Timothy. We are writing to the church in Thessalonica, to you who belong to God the Father and the Lord Jesus Christ. May God give you grace and peace. (1 Thessalonians 1:1 NLT)

This letter is from Paul, Silas, and Timothy. We are writing to the church in Thessalonica, to you who belong to God our Father and the Lord Jesus Christ. (2 Thessalonians 1:1 NLT)

This letter is from Paul, a prisoner for preaching the Good News about Christ Jesus, and from our brother Timothy. I am writing to Philemon, our beloved co-worker. (Philemon 1:1 NLT)

Servant leader—He served faithfully

But you know how Timothy has proved himself. Like a son with his father, he has served with me in preaching the Good News. (Philippians 2:22 NLT)

Missionary—He participated in the second missionary journey of the church

3 So Paul wanted him [Timothy] to join them on their journey. In deference to the Jews of the area, he arranged for Timothy to be circumcised before they left, for everyone knew that his father was a Greek. 4 Then they went from town to town, instructing the believers to follow the decisions made by the apostles and elders in Jerusalem. (Acts 16:3-4 NLT)

Messenger—He was sent to deliver messages and visited churches

That's why I have sent Timothy, my beloved and faithful child in the Lord. He will remind you of how I follow Christ Jesus, just as I teach in all the churches wherever I go. (1 Corinthians 4:17 NLT)

If the Lord Jesus is willing, I hope to send Timothy to you soon for a visit. Then he can cheer me up by telling me how you are getting along. (Philippians 2:19 NLT)

But now Timothy has just returned, bringing us good news about your faith and love. He reports that you always remember our visit with joy and that you want to see us as much as we want to see you. (1 Thessalonians 3:6 NLT)

Teacher—Paul emphasized the importance of teaching to Timothy

If you explain these things to the brothers and sisters, Timothy, you will be a worthy servant of Christ Jesus, one who is nourished by the message of faith and the good teaching you have followed. (1 Timothy 4:6)

Teach these things and insist that everyone learn them. (1 Timothy 4:11)

Until I get there, focus on reading the Scriptures to the church, encouraging the believers, and teaching them. (1 Timothy 4:13)

Keep a close watch on how you live and on your teaching. Stay true to what is right for the sake of your own salvation and the salvation of those who hear you. (1 Timothy 4:16)

Preacher—He advised Timothy to be always ready to preach the Word

Preach the word of God. Be prepared, whether the time is favorable or not. Patiently correct, rebuke, and encourage your people with good teaching. (2 Timothy 4:2 NLT)

Evangelist–Paul trained Timothy to prioritize evangelism in ministry

But you be watchful in all things, endure afflictions, do the work of an evangelist, fulfill your ministry. (2 Timothy 4:5 NKJV)

Paul's second letter to Timothy

Paul wrote his second letter to Timothy when he was nearing his death in Rome. The letter was full of marks of kindness, tenderness, and final ministry instructions as he was handing over the baton. As you read it, especially the last chapter, you could sense that this was a letter full of mixed emotions. It was a sober but very emotional letter written to his dear disciple and is justly looked upon as the final written communication with him.

There was no time for a lot of words in this letter, nor another opportunity for one more letter, and Paul probably knew that this was his final communication with his beloved son who worked with him in ministry for years on this side of heaven. This letter was probably written just weeks before his death. Paul, like a true apostle who heard from God, foresaw his imminent departure from this earth coming, and he did not hold back his true feelings, emotions, and deepest desires. He sent the final instructions to his mentee, Timothy, a young man in whom he had invested all that he had and all that he knew.

Paul's final letter became so real, personal, and fulfilled before his very eyes. It was more than just a letter to Timothy, who was like a son to Paul. What we have here is one last love letter. Paul did not have a family. That was all forsaken for the gospel's sake. So he called Timothy his son, his beloved son to show him as his closest family.

Finally, Paul desired Timothy to come to Rome to see him before winter and bring with him several things which he'd left at Troas. If Timothy went to Rome, and it is likely that he did, he must have been an eyewitness of the martyrdom of his mentor, leader, and father figure, Paul. I imagine the pain and the anguish that Timothy went through after Paul's death.

Possibly Timothy read that letter again and again and again, day in and day out as he kept on with ministry work. Every time he felt like giving up or getting discouraged, he would pull it out and read the final part of the letter, just to be reminded of what his predecessor had finally instructed him to do. I am sure his spirit would get revived and recharged to keep on moving, no matter the circumstances.

The mentor's words could be very reviving and be the source of encouragement, as the mentee would hate to disappoint him and suffer the pain of regret. Timothy knew that Paul had invested all he had in life in this gospel, so he wanted to be the best recipient of the baton and run with it without fail.

Paul wrote this most passionate personal letter to make sure that Timothy would continue with the gospel of Jesus Christ. Paul was convinced that the gospel would continue until it reached the whole Afro-Eurasia transcontinental region called the Middle East, which included Western Asia, Egypt, and Turkey. We thank God that today, the gospel reached Europe, Asia, Africa, Australia, and North and South America. Paul spent years training Timothy and prepared him for this final moment. Paul was just writing a letter to Timothy, just like when you write a letter or an email to your cousin, teacher, student, pastor, brother, sister, or friend today. Paul probably didn't realize that the letter would still be treasured almost two thousand years later.

All he did was share some personal final words, advice, thoughts, and values with his son, Timothy. He did not envisage that it would reach you and me.

The following are the final emotional words that kept on ringing in Timothy's inner ears like a song on repeat day and night.

> *1 I solemnly urge you in the presence of God and Christ Jesus, who will someday judge the living and the dead when he comes to set up his Kingdom: 2 Preach the word of God. Be prepared, whether the time is favorable or not. Patiently correct, rebuke, and encourage your people with good teaching. 3 For a time is coming when people will no longer listen to sound and wholesome teaching. They will follow their own desires and will look for teachers who will tell them whatever their itching ears want to hear. 4 They will reject the truth and chase after myths. 5 But you should keep a clear mind in every situation. Don't be afraid of suffering for the Lord. Work at telling others the Good News, and fully carry out the ministry God has given you. 6 As for me, my life has already been poured out as an offering to God. The time of my death is near. 7 I have fought the good fight, I have finished the race, and I have remained faithful. 8 And now the prize awaits me the crown of righteousness, which the Lord, the righteous Judge, will give me on the day of his return. And the prize is not just for me but for all who eagerly look forward to his appearing. (2 Timothy 4:1-15 NLT)*

Paul wrote this final letter like an athlete who has just won a race in the Olympics and is using his last oomph of strength to run around the field tracks waving the flag of his country with pride. That one last lap is called the lap of victory. This letter was the lap of victory for Paul.

Timothy had seen a lot of battles, beatings, and trouble since the day he'd first met Paul. Paul made sure that he poured out everything that he had on Timothy. He encouraged Timothy to endure hardship, suffer for Christ, rightly divide the word, flee youthful desires, seek righteousness, faith, love, and peace. He also taught him to avoid foolish questions and arguments and to be gentle. These are exhortations from an apostle who was about to die to his spiritual son. I am convinced that the letter served as a motivation for Timothy to continue serving with greater intensity and follow in the footprints of his closest leader and predecessor.

With death so close, Paul must have emotionally thought about meeting the Lord Jesus. His appreciative mind must have gone back to the first time they met. He started reflecting on his first encounter with the Lord on the road to Damascus. How much had transpired since then, what a life he had lived. He must have deeply thought about Ananias, the first brother that he met in Damascus. His mind took him down memory lane, through his learning years, all the missionary journeys, the first time he met Timothy's family. He thought about the converts, the confrontations, shipwrecks, stonings, and beatings. There were also the joys and love of teaching and growing in the bonds of Christian love.

Finally, Paul confided to the one to whom he felt closest, and he opened up to him. He became vulnerable and shared his final moments and feelings with Timothy, and here are the triumphant words of Paul's lap of victory:

"6 For I am already being poured out as a drink offering, and the time of my departure is at hand. 7 I have fought the good fight, I have finished the race, I have kept the faith." (2 Timothy 4:6,7 NKJV)

Second chair leadership lessons learned from Timothy

Leadership development and discipleship is not an event, but an intentional process

The relationship between Paul and Timothy is a perfect example of how relationships in leadership can develop over time. It takes a lot of patience, sacrifice, passion, dedication, and deliberate investment to develop another leader. Effective mentoring in any organization, industry, ministry, church, or leadership environment needs long-term commitment. Unfortunately, few people are committed to investing their time and energy in mentoring. As much time as we spend desiring, praying, and looking for more laborers, we should also spend time investing in those with the potential to become our partners in the mission. Identify people from your own congregation and mentor them to the level of ministry leadership, just as Paul did with Timothy.

Every leader needs mentors and models

As a leader, you need other leaders just ahead of where you are in your growth and your journey. And every leader also needs to be mentoring and modeling those just behind us. This is the only way for discipleship to take on the multi-generational nature described by Paul in 2 Timothy 2:2.

Mentoring is a process

Mentoring is a three-step/phase process including parenting, modeling, and partnering. Paul was convinced that it was worth his time and effort to mentor Timothy. He demonstrated these three steps from the time he picked up Timothy in Lystra as a spiritual parent, then modeled how to do ministry during their missionary journey. He finally recognized Timothy as his ministry partner when he handed over the church and the work of ministry to Timothy. *"Timothy, my fellow worker, sends you his greetings."* (Romans 16:21 NLT) Our goal is not only to make one disciple for Jesus, but to make disciples who make disciples. Today, we are serving in the kingdom because of the repetition of this three-phase process for centuries. The process didn't stop with Timothy. The baton has been passed to you who are reading this book, and it is our responsibility to be parents, modelers, and partners with the next generation until Jesus comes.

Chapter 4
Joseph

This proposal pleased Pharaoh and all his servants. 38 And Pharaoh said to his servants, "Can we find a man like this, in whom is the Spirit of God?" 39 Then Pharaoh said to Joseph, "Since God has shown you all this, there is none so discerning and wise as you are. 40 You shall be over my house, and all my people shall order themselves as you command. Only as regards the throne will I be greater than you." 41 And Pharaoh said to Joseph, "See, I have set you over all the land of Egypt." 42 Then Pharaoh took his signet ring from his hand and put it on Joseph's hand, and clothed him in garments of fine linen and put a gold chain about his neck. (Genesis 41:37)

Joseph is one of my favorite characters in the Bible. His story is a tale of jealousy, deceit, slavery, misrepresentation, injustice, lust, rivalry, and fear, and closes with forgiveness and reconciliation. The story is a wonderful example of how life as we know it is not a straight line. Life is full of ups and downs, mountains and valleys, years of famine, and years of plenty. God worked in Joseph's life through all of its ups and downs. Alistair Begg summed it up well when he said that Joseph was a life-sized illustration of Romans 8:28 (NKJV): *"And we know that all things work together for good to those who love God, to those who are called according to His purpose."*

Joseph was the 11th of 12 sons of the wealthy nomad Jacob and his second wife Rachel. His story is told in the book of Genesis 37-50. Joseph was the most loved son of his father Jacob because he had been born to him in his old age. He was given a special gift by his father, the famous robe of many colors.

His story is one of heroic redemption and forgiveness. When Joseph reported having dreams of his brothers, and even the stars and moon, bowing before him, their jealousy of him grew into action. The brothers sold him into slavery to a traveling caravan of Ishmaelites who took him to Egypt and sold him to Potiphar, the captain of Pharaoh's guard. Potiphar's wife falsely accused him of attempted rape, and he was unjustly imprisoned. In Egypt, the Lord's presence with Joseph enabled him to find favor with Potiphar and the keeper of the prison. With God's help, Joseph interpreted the dreams of two prisoners who were Pharaoh's servants, he predicted that one of them would be reinstated but the other put to death. Two years later, Joseph was called to interpret the dreams of Pharaoh. The interpretation anticipated seven years of plenty followed by seven years of famine. At that point, Joseph emerged as the only one who would solve the famine problem for the king, by the way, he told the king that there would be famine in the land, and the solution was that the king should create a position for someone who would be closer to him as the chief administrator and take care of the coming famine. The king just turned around and said, "We don't need to interview anybody else for the job; you, Joseph, are the only one who qualifies." Joseph was immediately appointed as the prime minister of the whole country of Egypt.

Joseph created a position for himself while a prisoner; he even created the job description for himself. That is what we call God's favor. Pharaoh recognized Joseph's God-given ability and prompted his promotion from prison to the chief administrator of the whole country of Egypt.

As predicted, the shortage of food in Canaan forced Jacob to send his sons to buy grain from the Egyptians. Benjamin, Joseph's younger brother, remained at home as Jacob feared losing him, as he had Joseph. When Joseph finally encountered his brothers again, he deliberately concealed his identity. He accused them of being spies and told them that next time they should come with Benjamin or he would not sell them the grain. The ongoing famine forced Jacob to reluctantly send his sons back to Egypt with Benjamin, and they were unexpectedly invited to dine at Joseph's house. Joseph then tested the character of his brothers by placing a silver cup in the sack of Benjamin and falsely accused him of theft. When Judah offered to stay in place of Benjamin, Joseph knew that his character had changed and revealed that he was their brother. Joseph explained that they need not feel guilty for betraying him as it was God's plan for him to be in Egypt to preserve his family. He told them to bring their father and his entire household into Egypt to live in the province of Goshen because there were five more years of famine left. Joseph supplied them with Egyptian transport wagons, new garments, silver, and twenty additional donkeys carrying provisions for the journey. Jacob then joyously reunited with his son Joseph.

Second chair leadership lessons learned from the Joseph

Perseverance

Despite the many ups and downs in his life (sold into slavery, falsely accused of attempted rape by Potiphar's wife and imprisoned, forgotten in prison for two more years by the chief cupbearer), Joseph was faithful and never questioned God's plan for him. We are told throughout his story that the Lord was with him. This is a good lesson for all leaders who are going through many successes and failures in their lives. Do not lose hope, do not give up; the Lord is still with you even in your pain and challenges.

Character

Although he was spoiled by his father's favoritism, Joseph eventually grew into a man of character. I like the definition of character as being "Doing the right thing when nobody (but God) is watching." Joseph was handsome, and he could have easily given in to the temptation of Potiphar's wife. Nobody (but God) would have known. He resisted and ended up being sent to prison when he was falsely accused of attempted rape. May God help you as a leader to be a man or a woman of character who represents God even in dark places, during the day and at night.

Good work ethic

Throughout Joseph's life, in the house of Potiphar, in the prison, and as second in command in Egypt, we see that Joseph's good work was rewarded by the Lord. We are told that whatever

Joseph did, the Lord made it succeed. We should be dedicated to doing our very best in all that we are assigned to do, at work, home, church, and then let God bless it. As a leader, do your best in any ministry or project that you are requested to do and let God do the rest.

Humility

Joseph was a humble and respectful man. He always gave credit to God; he never took it for himself. For example, in Genesis 42:15-16, Pharaoh tells Joseph that he had a dream, and he'd heard that Joseph was able to interpret dreams. Rather than taking the credit, Joseph humbly and honestly states that it is not him, but God who will give Pharaoh a favorable answer. After a successful project or ministry work, do we sometimes take credit ourselves, rather than giving it to the Lord?

Just imagine how he felt when he was pulled out of the prison and inaugurated to oversee the whole country in one day. His fellow prisoners expected him to come back and join them as a prisoner but were surprised when he visited the prison as a man of authority. He stayed humble throughout his life. May God help us stay humble as Peter advises us. At the right time, He will lift us up.

Trustworthiness

Trustworthiness means to be reliable and dependable. Joseph was trustworthy and loyal. When tempted by Potiphar's wife, he would not betray Potiphar nor sin against God. Joseph was a very authentic leader. People want to be around people who are real, authentic, and have high character. Authentic people are not trying to be above anyone else. They are likable, humble, and easy to talk to. Trustworthy people are consistent, compassionate, kind, resourceful, humble, and available. I pray that we can have more trustworthy leaders like Joseph.

No Power Abuse

Unlike many leaders today, Joseph didn't abuse his power. As a second in command in Egypt, he could have denied food to his brothers, or even thrown them in prison. Instead, he demonstrated forgiveness to them. Many leaders today abuse their power in many different ways. Power abuse occurs when a leader acts in a manner that manipulates an area of control for personal gain at the expense of his followers. In addition, Joseph was a forgiving leader; he granted forgiveness to his brothers who abused him. Forgiveness is a wonderful characteristic of Christ-centered leaders.

Offense-proof heart

If ever there was a man who had all the rights and justification to stay offended, angry, and bitter, it was Joseph. However, he refused to be overcome by anger and bitterness. He chose forgiveness over bitterness. You can't lead with an offended heart. Jesus said He came to heal the brokenhearted. As much as it is difficult to walk with a broken leg or to carry things with a broken arm, it is difficult to lead well with a broken heart. It is very difficult to lead with an offended heart. Learn to forgive so that you can focus on your purpose. God brought Joseph earlier to Egypt so that he could preserve the nation of Israel. Just imagine what could have happened if Joseph chose to be a leader who stayed offended.

Chapter 5
Aaron

*13 But Moses said, "Pardon your servant, Lord. Please send
someone else." 14 Then the Lord's anger burned against
Moses, and he said, "What about your brother, Aaron
the Levite? I know he can speak well. He is already on
his way to meet you, and he will be glad to see you. 15
You shall speak to him and put words in his mouth; I
will help both of you speak and will teach you what to
do. 16 He will speak to the people for you, and it will be
as if he were your mouth and as if you were God to
him." (Exodus 4:13-16 NLT)*

The children of Israel went to Egypt when their father Jacob
was invited by his son Joseph. Now God wanted to release them
from slavery. Moses was born to set them free and lead them to
the promised land. Aaron was the older brother of Moses. They
grew up in extremely different circumstances. Moses grew up in
a royal household, while his brother Aaron grew up as a slave.
His first 83 years were spent in Egyptian bondage. They
separated after Moses ran away from Pharaoh after he killed an
Egyptian who was beating up an Israelite. He settled down in the
land of Midian, where he met Jethro and Zipporah. God reunited
them later in life. They worked together to lead the Hebrews out
of Egypt and to the Promised Land.

Aaron is first mentioned in the Bible when God
communicated with Moses in the burning bush. Aaron was the
older brother of Moses. In his initial encounter with the Lord

during this burning bush experience, Moses was not eager to accept God's call to lead Israel out of Egypt to the Promised Land. Instead, Moses pleaded, "please send someone else." Moses was reluctant to accept the mission to free them from the Egyptian oppression. God ignored his plea and sent him on his way to Egypt to lead Israel, estimated at about two million people, to the promised land.

Because Moses complained that he could not speak well, God assigned Aaron, his brother, as his assistant and spokesman, thereby creating a team of two brothers. God told him that Aaron was a good speaker and that he would be his second chair leader. Moses had a challenge with communication; possibly he could not communicate well in the Egyptian language and Hebrew language because he'd left the country about 40 years earlier. Aaron, his brother, had stayed in Egypt for all that time, was fluent in both languages, and was a good fit to help and support his brother. He acted as a middleman between Moses and the Hebrews.

God confirmed Aaron's communication skills when He said to Moses, "What about your brother, Aaron the Levite? I know he can speak well. He will speak to the people for you, and it will be as if he were your mouth and as if you were God to him."

There is no self-sufficient leader. Aaron functioned as Moses' assistant; every leader needs an assistant or more. The two brothers were already old men when they reunited and started working together as a team. Aaron was 83 years old, and Moses was 80 years old when Pharaoh finally yielded to their request and let the Israelites go. They worked as a team for 40 years, and they complemented each other. Aaron was 123 years old when he died on Mount Hor, near the southern end of the Dead Sea.

Today, everyone who is anointed wants to be the main leader. I wonder how many would be willing to serve under one leader so faithfully for 40 years. Remember, Moses was Aaron's younger brother, but Aaron was willing to submit to him. Aaron was a better communicator than Moses; however, he did not allow his pride to overshadow him and undermine Moses. He served under him for 40 years. For all those years, he daily assisted Moses in leading Israel. Aaron provided spiritual leadership to the nation. He was a very devout, good, and spiritual man. For 40 years he served as the High Priest of God's people.

After the march out of Egypt, Aaron was no longer a central figure in the events but only a secondary player at Moses' side. He didn't play any important part in the crossing of the Red Sea, the songs of victory hymns, or the water crisis at Marah. He reappeared later in connection with the incident of the manna.

He held up the arms of Moses as they were fighting against the Amalekites. The other notable moments that Aaron played a role in the success of his brother is recorded in Exodus 17. It is recorded that during the battle between the Israelites and the Amalekites, Aaron, together with Hur, supported Moses' hands stretched upward to ensure victory.

Aaron modeled an assistant leader who is always supportive of his leader. He supported and stood by his brother when he was facing the hardhearted Pharaoh. He persisted and stayed loyal to Moses even when some of Israel rebelled against him. Later, again with Hur, in Exodus 32, Aaron acted as deputy for Moses when his brother climbed Mount Sinai to receive the two stone tablets of the Law. He was a faithful helper to his brother Moses. He was a leader who was always committed to his people. Aaron was a leader who was quick to obey God; his obedience was displayed in his initial call to join Moses.

He responded positively and immediately when he was called to lead the Israelites out of Egypt, and his faithfulness during the long years of wilderness is exemplary.

He understood his position and responsibilities as the assistant leader, and he augmented Moses' leadership with his communication skills. As an assistant, you are not there to compete with but to complement your senior leader. Sometimes you may stay invisible to the public as Aaron did. As long you have the heart to serve, God will bless you for that. There could be some skills or gifts that you are good at or things that you could do much better than your leader, but be willing to submit and serve. There is no leader who knows how to do everything; leaders should accept any help that God brings to their lives for the sake of the ministry. We thank God for exemplary leaders like Moses. If Moses and Aaron could function as a team, anyone can.

Second chair leadership lessons learned from Aaron

Even the best leaders make mistakes

Aaron was obedient most of his life; he followed God throughout. However, he had moments where he did not do God's will. Aaron was far from being perfect; however, this didn't keep him from serving as Moses' spokesman and right-hand man. You and I are not perfect, but there is still a place for us in God's kingdom. In Exodus 32 we read of a situation where Aaron missed it.

When Moses went to Mount Sinai to collect the commandments from God, he put Aaron in charge of leading the nation of Israel. Instead of leading people to worship God, the people started doubting God and started to believe in man-made gods. Aaron failed to direct the people toward the truth. He consented to the people and joined them in their doubt of God. They built a golden calf to worship in place of God. Aaron allowed sin and chaos to enter the camp.

If Aaron was serving under some of the leaders today, he would have been fired for making such a big blunder. However, God and Moses saw something different than what we could see in him. God saw in Aaron a destiny for the children of Israel. Instead of just seeing leadership toward evil, God saw a man who would lead the nation into the promised land. He did not demote Aaron but redirected his talents for His own glory.

Faithful servant leadership leads to legacy

Aaron became the first high priest of Israel. God chose him and set him apart. Aaron became the first example of priestly holiness. Instead of seeing only failure, God saw the future of His nation in him. Despite his sins and shortcomings, Aaron was used by God to fill a special and important role in the nation of Israel. You and I are not perfect, but there is still a place for us in God's kingdom. Do not get discouraged by your failures and shortcomings. God's gracious forgiveness is able to erase your failures.

Beware of manipulation

The world is full of leaders who evade responsibility and shift the blame when things go wrong. As a leader, you have to make sure that you do not get manipulated into acting against God's will. After being manipulated, Aaron stood and blamed the people and the fire. "They gave me the gold, we threw it into the fire, and this calf came out of the fire." Your leadership matters at every level of the organization. It is your leadership responsibility to reroute the church or organization when it moves in the wrong direction. Your leadership will determine the health and the direction of the church. Leadership matters; there is a direct correlation between the spiritual health of the people and the spiritual health of their leaders.

Chapter 6
Elisha

So Elisha returned to his oxen and slaughtered them. He used the wood from the plow to build a fire to roast their flesh. He passed around the meat to the townspeople, and they all ate. Then he went with Elijah as his assistant. (1 Kings 19:21 NLT)

As they were walking along and talking, suddenly a chariot of fire appeared, drawn by horses of fire. It drove between the two men, separating them, and Elijah was carried by a whirlwind into heaven. 12 Elisha saw it and cried out, "My father! My father! I see the chariots and charioteers of Israel!" And as they disappeared from sight, Elisha tore his clothes in distress. 13 Elisha picked up Elijah's cloak, which had fallen when he was taken up. Then Elisha returned to the bank of the Jordan River. (2 Kings 2:11-13 NLT)

The story of Elijah and Elisha may be the most obvious mentorship story in the Bible. It tells us much about both the role of the mentor and the mentee. In his first encounter with Elijah, Elisha was willing to let go of his occupation, his family, and the life he had built over the years in order to follow after a man offering his mentorship. He killed his oxen and destroyed the yoke, giving the proceeds to his neighborhood. He literally did not want to put his hands to the plow anymore. This would be the equivalent of selling a business and throwing a party with the proceeds. He did all this to leave his leadership role in the field and become an assistant to the prophet.

Elisha left a position that had job security, benefits, and guaranteed income, and started following this prophet who was very unstable, sometimes fearful, and would run from Jezebel and be hated by some people who would not agree with his prophecy. Some people would see this as a demotion. When we move into God's purposes, we are not demoted but promoted. God knew what was awaiting him in the near future: He would experience the fulfillment and peace that no amount of money and job security could provide. Elisha was destined for a double portion. If he had never offered himself to serve under Elijah, he would have remained a farmer and never performed the amazing miracles that blessed the lives of so many others. Sometimes we fail to move to the next level of our purpose because of fear and the comfort zone of familiarity experience. If we want to experience God and reach our potential, we have to step out of the boat into the water, just like Peter did. There is no growth in our comfort zones.

Due to his willingness to serve under the man of God, Elisha was later promoted and became Elijah's substitute. After this incident, Elisha performed more miracles than Elijah did. When God calls you to His will, there is always something better than what you have, better than where you are, and more fulfilling than what you are doing now. Please do not resist when the Lord calls you to serve others. To the human eye, sometimes it may look like a demotion, but God sees much further ahead than we do. God knew what would happen six years later. Sometimes God would like you to serve under someone as He prepares your heart for your new role later. Learn to submit to the process and serve faithfully.

Bible scholars believe that Elisha served Elijah for six years before Elijah was ushered into heaven. At this time an interesting test was set before Elisha, and he passed it. Elijah three times told Elisha to stay behind, but each time Elisha refused to leave him. Others were watching from a distance, but Elisha wanted a close-up and personal view of what God was about to do in Elijah's life. Elisha was truly committed to serving under Elijah and did not allow any excuse to stop or discourage him. Those watching from a distance were not left with the double portion, only the one who served closely and persevered. There is no wasted experience with God. As you are serving under your leader, God could be preparing you for the next assignment. Sometimes it will be challenging, and you may feel like quitting and go back to plowing, but please do not despise your small beginnings. God has more for you, so continue to serve under your Elijah.

Spangler and Tverberg in their book, *Sitting at the Feet of the Rabbi Jesus,* wrote a lot about the subject of Jewish discipleship. One of the interesting ideas that they explained was that Jesus used "the plow of Elisha" in Luke 9 as the model for how he expected his own disciples to be committed to Him above everything else. *"61 Another said, 'Yes, Lord, I will follow you, but first let me say good-bye to my family.' 62 But Jesus told him, 'Anyone who puts a hand to the plow and then looks back is not fit for the Kingdom of God.' Jesus replied, 'No one who puts his hand to the plow and looks back is fit for service in the kingdom of God."* (Luke 9:61-62)

There are a lot of similarities between Elijah and Jesus in the way they trained their disciples. Several aspects of Elisha's life exemplified discipleship in Jesus' time. Elisha joined Elijah and lived with him full-time for many years. The end goal was not just academic learning but real personal transformation. It was through this prolonged intimacy with his teacher that Elisha learned the full significance of the ministry. He learned more and understood ministry more through his close association with his leader.

When the Lord called Samuel, he was living in the same household with his leader and trainer, Eli. The boy Samuel ministered before the Lord under Eli. Samuel was working as the servant of Eli, Israel's chief priest, who was now very old. It was Eli who had the responsibility to teach Samuel and prepare him to become the next prophet in the land. Eli was the high priest of Shiloh and the second-to-last Israelite judge. Eli was later succeeded by Samuel before the rule of the first of the Kings of Israel and Judah came in. Samuel anointed the first two kings of Israel, Saul, and David. Eli was able to help Samuel identify the voice of the Lord and how he should respond. Discipleship involves modeling how one could hear from God and how he should respond. Eli had a great impact on Samuel because he lived with him day and night.

The disciples did not visit Jesus during a church service, healing service, or special occasions. They lived with Him full time. They would accompany Him on all of his daily rounds, they saw Him relate with His family, rejected by His brothers, heal the sick, feed the hungry, help the poor, raise the dead, and so on, that impacted them more than if He would preach and then disappear after the sermon.

Jesus' disciples also served Him; they would help Him with some errands when He asked them to. Sometimes they would go to town to buy food (John 4:8). He would send them to go and pay for him. *"27 However, we don't want to offend them, so go down to the lake and throw in a line. Open the mouth of the first fish you catch, and you will find a large silver coin.[d] Take it and pay the tax for both of us."* (Matthew 17:27) At times He asked them to arrange for the

Passover celebration according to His directions (Luke 22:8). As they were moving from place to place, the disciples were expected to take turns preparing the meals and serve each other. They learned to serve one another from Jesus himself. He would always remind them that He did not come to be served, but to serve. He would even remind them that the greatest in the kingdom is the one who serves others. He would demonstrate this principle practically by washing their feet. They did not hear Him preach a powerful sermon then vanish and appear again the next day. He lived with them; they saw Him live the gospel that He preached. So the teacher-disciple relationship was very strong and intimate. In that sense, Jesus was not doing anything new from what Elijah and Elisha did.

God brings people closer to you so they can learn from you. God wants you to model your leadership in real life to them. Living the gospel is totally different from verbally preaching it. Let your mentee see you go through the challenges of life and how you handle them. Let them know you are a real person with the same challenges that they are facing, and that you handle them in a Christian way. Let them see you trust God for meeting your needs or leading you through the difficult time or financial challenges in your life.

Second chair leadership lessons learned from Elisha

Busy people make the best leaders

Elijah found Elisha in the field working hard. He was obviously a man of means because he was plowing with 12 yokes of oxen ahead of him. However, when Elijah called him, he left them to serve Elijah. God calls busy people to lead His people. I am sure if Elijah had found Elisha just idling around doing nothing, he wouldn't have invited him into his ministry. People who do nothing will not start to do something just because now they have a position. Peter, James, and John were already fishermen when Jesus called them. If you want to get a great successor as a leader, identify someone who is already doing something with his life. One of the problems that lead to the failure of most governments is that they give responsibilities to people who have no idea of what they are doing. Some are given positions just because they are comrades and friends with no experience or knowledge of what is expected of them. The person who is already in the field views your invitation to leadership as an expansion of what he is already doing. He may not be doing exactly what you are doing, just like Elisha who was farming, but he was already busy doing something with his life. Lazy people will not instantly turn and become industrious just because they are given a position in the organization, church, or company.

When you look for your successor, you should look to those who have demonstrated the ability to be successful in some other areas of their lives or ministry.

True leadership is costly

Great decisions in life call for a sacrifice. In order to become the best second chair leader that he was, Elisha made two big sacrifices. The first sacrifice was when he immediately followed Elijah without even telling his family or parents about what had happened. This could mean that he immediately cut off all his family ties. We are not sure of the reason for him to do so; all we know is that he was not permitted to go back and say goodbye to his family. The second sacrifice is the killing of the oxen. Oxen were very valuable because of their labor ability. Killing them would be a great financial loss to him and his family.

There are times when we are called to make sacrifices for deciding to walk in our purpose. We may not necessarily have to make the same sacrifices that Elisha did; however, we also may need to sacrifice something, it could be our comfort, time, energy, finances, or even some relationships that may not be supportive of our vision. Leadership is not cheap.

Great leaders replace themselves

Elijah knew that he had to prepare a successor. Great leaders do not make members; they make other leaders. From day one as a leader, you should prepare someone to take over your leadership position. Responsible leaders pass their authority to the potential leader. No leader is successful until he has a successor. The success of your leadership ability is only seen after you have stepped aside from the leadership position. The potential leader stays close to the leader so he can learn from the leader and grow.

Developing other leaders around you will also help you deal with the challenge that most leaders have, loneliness. It is said the higher you go, the colder it becomes. It is true, it is sometimes lonely up there because as leaders, your time to fellowship and socialize is so limited due to a compact schedule. Just because you might feel alone doesn't mean you are alone. One way to make sure of this is to do leadership with someone. You have a lot of experience and knowledge that you can share with others. You may organize regular leadership development training sessions with the leaders that you have influence over. Whether you are a first or second chair leader, find someone who doesn't know what you know and teach them. In ministry, never do anything alone. I have learned a lot in leadership when I traveled with my leaders and managers to different churches and institutions throughout the country and internationally. It is always advisable to take someone with you when you do ministry work. You can invite someone when you go to the hospital for a visit or when visiting someone's house. It is also okay to share your sermon or discuss it with someone as you plan for your next speaking engagement. You will be surprised how much the person will learn from you. Just expose other people to ministry. You have a lot to offer to those around you; I sure it's far more than you ever imagined. Remember, what's obvious to you is amazing to others. As leaders, we should be in the business of replacing ourselves. My question to you is: Who are you pouring into?

Chapter 7
John Mark

When he realized this, he went to the home of Mary, the mother of John Mark, where many were gathered for prayer. 13 He knocked at the door in the gate, and a servant girl named Rhoda came to open it. (Acts 12:12)

John Mark served as a second chair leader throughout his life. As a young man, John Mark is first mentioned as the son of a well-to-do woman named Mary. Possibly, Mary had a big house in Jerusalem, where she could accommodate the whole church for their regular meetings. They held their church services and regular prayer meetings at her house. John Mark was a very obscure biblical figure; he was just a regular young man serving under other ministers.

Just like Saul, whose other name was Paul and Simon, who was also called Peter, John also had two names; he was also known as Mark. This is because it was common for Jews of that period to bear both a Semitic name such as John (Hebrew: Yochanon, meaning "Yahweh is gracious"), and a Greco-Roman name (Marcus, or Mark). The name John points to his Jewish heritage, and Mark served as his second name.

After the angel of the Lord miraculously released Peter from jail, he went straight to Mary's house. The fact that upon his miraculous release from prison, Peter knew where to find the praying church implies that Mary held a position of some prominence among the early Jewish Christian church in

Jerusalem.

There is no direct information concerning the early life of Mark. However, deducing from the fact that Peter was welcomed at the house of Mary and from information in the first epistle, Peter appears to have been well known to Mark. Apparently, over the course of time, Mark became even closer to Peter as he ministered throughout Asia Minor and Rome. By the time Peter wrote this first epistle, Mark had become like a son to him. *"Your sister church here in Babylon sends you greetings, and so does my son Mark."* (1 Pet 5:13)

John Mark was not one of the apostles of Jesus. However, he spent a lot of time with Peter and learned a lot about the life of Jesus from him. He was so blessed to have the firsthand narration of the life of Jesus by a man who was in the inner circle of Jesus' ministry. He was so blessed to grow in the presence of the great Apostle who intimately knew and lived with Jesus for three years. John Mark served as Peter's scribe and notetaker. He would listen to Peter share his personal experiences with Jesus, and I could imagine Peter kept repeating and emphasizing some stories in almost every preaching. Peter would always share his testimony about his first encounter with Jesus in the Sea of Galilee. Seeing how Jesus took an uneducated, sinful man and loved him infinitely gave Mark hope and great assurance.

John Mark was first mentioned in order to rightly identify his mother Mary, as she had a very popular name. Paul also indirectly mentioned Mary's relationship with Barnabas. In Colossians 4:10 he mentioned that John Mark was Barnabas' cousin. According to Acts 4:36-37, Barnabas was a Levite, a native of Cyprus, and a landowner. We can use deductive reasoning to conclude that Mary was possibly a Levite as well. Being a Levite, she would have loved to see her son serve in ministry too.

The household of Mary is pictured as being of considerable means: They had at least one servant girl and sufficient space to accommodate a sizable prayer meeting. Not everyone could afford to hire a servant. Nothing is said or known about his father, however, and since the house is called Mary's, we can assume that possibly he was dead by this time.

The first significant event regarding him as an assistant was when Paul and Barnabas returned to Antioch from their famine relief mission to Jerusalem. On their way back from Jerusalem to Antioch, they brought John Mark along with them as a ministry assistant. *"When Barnabas and Saul had finished their mission to Jerusalem, they returned, taking John Mark with them."* (Acts 12:25)

About a year later, the Holy Spirit appointed Paul and Barnabas from the Church at Antioch to go out and preach the gospel. Paul and Barnabas again asked John Mark to go out with them on their first missionary journey. Mark went with them as their ministry helper (Acts 13:5). Unfortunately, he did not complete the first missionary journey with them. Mark left the two senior men at Perga, the capital of the region of Artemis in Pamphylia, and returned to Jerusalem (Acts 13:13). The Bible does not say why Mark deserted them, but his departure came right after a mostly fruitless time on the island of Cyprus. Cyprus is the island where Barnabas originally came from. Only one conversion is recorded in Cyprus, but there had been strong demonic opposition by Bar-Jesus. It's likely that the young John Mark was discouraged at the hardness of the way and decided to return to the comforts of his home. It is not clear why he decided to go back home. Some suggested that he was overwhelmed by the work of ministry, and some suggest that he missed his mother back home in Jerusalem. The Bible does not say how he left, but some suggest that he possibly left or disappeared at night.

Sometime later, after Paul and Barnabas had returned from their first journey, Paul expressed a desire to go back to the brethren in the cities they had previously visited to see how everyone was doing (Acts 15:36). Barnabas agreed, but under one condition: He suggested that they take John Mark with them. Paul refused to take Mark with them on their second trip, citing his previous desertion. Paul thought it best not to have a quitter with them; they needed someone more dependable. Barnabas wanted to give his cousin John Mark a second chance. Barnabas, the "son of encouragement" (Acts 4:36), desired to forgive John Mark's failure and to give him another chance. Paul took the more rational view that pioneering missionary work requires dedication, resolve, and endurance.

Paul and Barnabas had a "sharp disagreement" about John Mark. This disagreement led to their separating from each other and going on separate journeys. Barnabas took John Mark with him back to his home island, Cyprus, and Paul took Silas with him through Syria and Cilicia to encourage the believers in those areas (Acts 15:39–41). From chapter 15 of the book of Acts onwards we never hear of Paul and Barnabas again, although we see Paul and Silas working together in ministry. Paul saw John Mark as a risk to their mission. It's worth noting that, in the end, two groups of missionaries were sent out to spread the gospel.

The Pauline correspondence indicates that within a decade or so of the rift over Mark, the relationship between Paul and Mark had improved greatly. In Colossians 4:10 Paul includes Mark among the few ministry co-workers who labored with him and provided him with some little comfort. Mark appears to have been chosen by the great Apostle Paul to make some representation to Colossae. Paul makes further mention of Mark; he calls him his "fellow worker" in Philemon 1:24.

By the time of the writing of his letter to Timothy, Mark and Timothy were together. Paul expressed his final, gratifying tribute for the young man. Near the end of his life, from a Roman prison, Paul sent a request to Timothy: *"Get Mark and bring him with you, because he is helpful to me in my ministry."* (2 Timothy 4:11) Obviously, John Mark had matured through the years and had become a faithful servant of the Lord. Paul recognized his progress and considered him a valuable companion.

According to the early church, Mark the Evangelist was the first bishop of Alexandria, Egypt, and the first person to establish a Christian church in that city. He also established many more churches around the Alexandria area.

None of the 12 apostles was as close to Jesus as Peter, James, and John. Serving under the leadership of one of these three could be the closest one could get to Jesus and his ministry. Peter would always repeat his experiences with Jesus from the day he met him for the first time in the sea of Galilee when he requested to use his boat. He would share the miracle of the biggest catch as the fisherman. He would tell them of this simple fisherman who was an ordinary man with no education, no value or stature in the community, but he was invited to become an apostle of Christ. Mark would listen so attentively as Peter told the churches about how he was able to get the revelation of Christ as the Messiah when they were in Caesarea. Peter would make sure that he did not miss the transfiguration experience every time he spoke. He repeatedly shared the testimony about the miraculous healing of his mother-in-law, the feeding of the crowds, the painful Gethsemane experience, the crucifixion, and the resurrection of his master. Due to his close proximity with Peter, their relationship developed over the years of working in ministry together. John Mark kept on recording all these eyewitnesses' experiences.

John Mark eventually recorded Peter's account of Jesus' life and ministry in what today is known as the gospel of Mark. In fact, since the whole gospel is Peter's narration of his life in ministry with Jesus, some scholars call it The Gospel According to Apostle Peter. Mark wrote this gospel that bears his name sometime between AD 55 and 59. It is believed that his gospel was the first to be composed. Mark was the first one to compose the story of Jesus as we know it today. He wrote about everything that he heard from Peter. He heard Peter keep repeating his experiences everywhere he went to preach. By the time he wrote the gospel, Mark knew what had actually happened throughout the ministry of Jesus. His gospel recorded Peter's account of Jesus' life and ministry. Mark's Gospel is an accurate record of Peter's teachings.

His writings were used as a source of reference for the gospels of Matthew and Luke. His writings will always be in the bibliography of the synoptic gospels. The synoptic gospels (Matthew, Mark, and Luke) cover most of the same miracles, parables, and events of Jesus' life and ministry. The book of John is different from the synoptic gospels; actually, there are no parables in his book.

Second chair leadership lessons learned from John Mark

You can leave a life-changing legacy, even as a second chair leader

John Mark was never a first chair leader. He was not even in the leadership structure of the church in Jerusalem or Antioch. He never led even a single mission trip. He never led any department, committee, or subcommittee but made a lifelong impact that we are still enjoying today. The gospel of Mark will always remain relevant and impactful in our lives and many generations to come. He was always an assistant to Peter, Paul, and his cousin Barnabas. Actually, even when his name was mentioned for the first time, it was not about him; the author was identifying his mother. You do not need to be famous or to be in the top leadership to make a significant difference. Jesus says the one who is great in ministry is the one who focuses on serving, not on making a big name for himself. The more you focus on serving, the more the Lord will lift you at the right time.

Man's rejection is not God's rejection

John Mark was rejected by Paul, who thought Mark would amount to nothing. He thought he was not fit for ministry; he never saw any future for him. Not everyone may understand your purpose. Sometimes even the people you look up to may fail to recognize and understand your purpose. Paul rejected Mark because he didn't recognize his calling. The same John Mark, the reject, finally played a big role in the writing of today's Bible and the establishment of the church in Africa. You might be rejected by your family, your spouse, your co-workers, your church, or even by your pastor or senior leader. Their rejection doesn't mean God has rejected you. You can still be like Mark and fulfill your calling in spite of their rejection.

Do not allow your past failures and disappointments to limit you

John Mark failed; however, he never gave up. He failed to complete the journey with Paul and Barnabas, but he completed the Gospel of Mark. He did not complete what Paul expected him to complete, but he completed what God expected him to complete—he completed his purpose. You may fail to meet people's expectations but still, meet God's expectations. You may fail to do what people expect you to do but still do what you are born for. People may label you and call you a failure, but God sees a John Mark and a giant in you. God sees a conqueror in you, not a failure. You should refuse people's labels and focus on accomplishing your calling. God has the best definition of who you are, so trust and believe Him, not people. Your true identity is with God, not man. Mark continued to focus on his purpose rather than his failures. Sometimes we focus so much on our failures, disappointments, defeats, and frustrations we allow those failures to define us. John Mark refused to be called a failure. He did not allow one event to define his whole life. Your life is bigger than that one event. When you fail, it does not mean you are a failure; it only means that you have failed in one situation. You can still be successful in the other areas of your life. Ask God to show you your purpose for living and continue to focus on it persistently.

When you fail, it simply means you have learned how not to do it. Continue to focus on the vision and the purpose that God has given you, even if it means you have to change the route to achieve it. Be stubborn with your vision but flexible with your methods. Be willing to compromise the methods but not your principles. Never allow failure to throw you off course. All successful people that you know of today have failed at some point in their lives. Study the biographies and the testimonies of the people that you consider successful in ministry, business, leadership, sports, or any area of life. They all have one thing in common: All of them have failed at some point in their lives. The only difference between successful and unsuccessful people is that whenever they fail, successful people do not give up. They keep on trying until they make it, whereas unsuccessful people just give up. This applies in all areas of life, whether private or public. Please be like John Mark—be persistent, do not give up on your dreams.

Not everyone may finish the journey with you

When you are a leader, you have to understand that all people come to your ministry for a reason, and some only for a season. Life is a series of seasons, and all seasons are temporal. In every season of your life, there are particular people that you need. When the student is ready, the teacher will show up. There was a season when Paul needed Mark; however, there was also a season when he did not need him. There came a time when he needed him again. God connects us and reconnects us with some people for a purpose. Some come to our lives for a lesson that God wants us to learn at that point. Some come to your life to help you grow in some areas of your life, like patience, forgiveness, faith, and relationship building.

Some people will be in your life to help you start your project or ministry; however, it does not mean they will finish with you. Don't get disappointed when some people desert you as Mark did with Paul and Barnabas. Maybe it was time for John Mark to reconnect with Peter, so God was preparing him to write the Gospel of Mark. If he'd stayed with Paul, he would not have had an opportunity to travel with Peter. Before you condemn someone, you need to check with God. As God is busy working in your heart, He is also working on the other person's heart. Not all situations are about you. We have to learn to approach all situations with open hearts and minds. Be willing to learn from all situations, both good and bad. In life, disappointments come when people do not do what we expected them to do. Some people may leave you when you do not expect them to leave and join other ministries. Remember, it is not always about you.

When the children of Israel rejected the leadership of Samuel's sons, Samuel thought they were rejecting him as they wanted a king. God assured him that they are not rejecting him. It was not about him.

"And the Lord told him: 'Listen to all that the people are saying to you; it is not you they have rejected, but they have rejected me as their king.'" (1 Samuel 8:7)

Some will leave you when you feel like you need them the most, but maybe God wants you to start trusting Him more for meeting your needs than them. Life is a series of seasons. There are people who will be good for you at a particular season, and when their season is over, they will leave, and rightly so. Do not feel rejected; it is not all about you. You are not the center of the universe; maybe at that point, there are other people who need them more than you. You should also understand that God brought them to your life to learn whatever He wanted them to learn; maybe it is time for them to move to the next chapter of their lives. I think by now you are aware that you do not know everything. There are things that you also are learning from other people. Some came to motivate and encourage you to study, but by the time you graduate they may no longer be there even to celebrate with you. Some may come to encourage you to write a book, but by the time you launch it, they may longer be there to celebrate with you. Not everyone may finish the journey with you, and it is not always wrong.

Grace is more powerful than revenge

Barnabas was willing to give John Mark a second chance. He understood that people may fail you sometimes, but you do not have to give up on them. As a leader, you need to learn to give people who failed you a second chance, or more. All of us have disappointed God many times, but as the Bible says, "He will never leave us nor forsake us." Be willing to give people a second chance. Peter understood John Mark very well when he returned from the mission trip. He welcomed him back because he understood that there is more power in grace than condemnation and revenge. Peter experienced the same guilt feeling that Mark experienced before—do you remember that Peter rejected Christ three times?

After His resurrection, Jesus found Peter fishing, and He asked him a heart-piercing question. "Simon, Simon, do you love me?" This was an introspective question for Peter. People only see what you do, but God knows and focuses on your heart, He focuses on why you do what you do. The motive for what you do is important to God. Jesus knew what was in Peter's heart.

Peter felt the guilt of rejecting his master, and said, "Yes, Lord, you know that I love you." Jesus told him, "Feed my sheep." He was telling Peter that "after you have been forgiven and given grace, go and give others the same grace and forgiveness that I gave you."

Having gone through this baptism of forgiveness, there is no way Peter would be harsh with Mark. He had to practice what he was instructed to do. Peter became more gracious than judgmental. We should be willing to give people grace rather than revenge or judgment.

Unlike Peter and Barnabas, Paul held a grudge against John Mark for many years; he took time to forgive him. Thank God that He eventually changed his heart about John Mark. People will always offend us, and at some point, we may even separate for a while. Great leaders are forgiving leaders. We should use every opportunity that we get to reconcile with them. Actually, the Bible says we have been given the ministry of reconciliation.

See potential in people

Paul did not see any potential in Mark. Sometimes young people will blunder and make mistakes. They will not always do it right. You have to decide to believe in them, have faith in them, believe that they have the potential to change, and do what God brought them here to do.

People will always offend us and disappoint us; however, we should not give up on them. No matter how they behave today, they have the potential to change. I have met pastors who have shared their testimonies with me, and some of the things that they did when they were still young. If God was to use our human myopic standards and judgments, their past sins and ungodly lives could have disqualified them from becoming pastors or even serving in ministry. God is not only a God of a second chance but many chances. All of us have blown our second chances a long time ago, but He remains gracious with us.

Everyone that God brings to your life has a purpose, and they will definitely fulfill it. They all have the potential to do exploits for the Kingdom of God. We should believe in the people that we lead. Sometimes it is those people that you underestimate who will make a significant difference in your organization, church, and the world. Maybe some of those that you least expect are destined to be your successor in ministry or your position.

Prayer changes things

John Mark was a young man who grew up in a house of prayer. The prayer of his mother played a big role later in his life; it kept him going as he left Jerusalem with Paul and Barnabas. Her prayer kept him going as he was serving in the church in Antioch, and the same prayer kept him when they traveled to Cyprus. When they crossed over to Perga, I am sure his mother continued to pray for him even when he deserted ministry for a while. The power of prayer was with him when he was serving under the Apostle Peter's ministry. Prayer kept him through when he wrote the Gospel of Mark. It was prayer that kept him in Africa when he started the church. He made some blunders in his life, but I believe it was the persistent prayers of Mary that sustained him. Never stop praying for your family, your children, and everyone you work with.

There is power in prayer. Let your children see you pray about any situation that concerns you. When they see God answer your prayers, their faith will be strengthened. Prayer has the power to change situations, things and lives, so do not stop praying for your loved ones. Some prayers may not be answered in your lifetime. When Steven was stoned to death by Paul's companions, he prayed a powerful prayer of faith. *"Lord, do not hold this sin against them."* (Acts 7:60) God answered his prayer later after his death. In Acts 9, Paul's sins were finally forgiven as Steven prayed just before he died.

Do not give up even when it looks like God is not answering your prayer. I can imagine the disappointment that John Mark's mother could have felt when he showed up at home and told her that he did not complete the trip, he did not make it in ministry. I am sure she kept on praying that God would help Mark discover his purpose on earth. I do not know if she was still alive when he finally wrote the Gospel of Mark. I am sure she would have been the most excited and thankful mother on earth, just to see her prayers being answered after almost 30 years. People that we pray for may continue to disappoint us and seem like they continue to live against our prayers or continue to do what is wrong; however, do not give up. Keep praying.

PART C

The Role of a Second Chair Leader

He makes the whole body fit together perfectly. As each part does its own special work, it helps the other parts grow, so that the whole body is healthy and growing and full of love. (Ephesians 4:16)

The second chair leader has a role to play in ministry growth. There are things that your main leader or pastor would do; however, as a leader, you also have some expectations to meet. When your leader does his part, and you also do your part, there will always be progress and growth. I have learned in life that if we keep doing the right thing, no matter how long it takes, the right results will follow. The following are some of the things that a second chair leader is expected to understand and do:

- Understand the limits of your authority
- Submission
- Move from dependency to interdependency
- Teamwork makes the team work
- Manage the contentment–dreaming tension
- Leave a legacy
- See your senior leader as a gift from God
- Leave the church the right way

Chapter 8
Understand the Limits of Your Authority

Leadership is influence, not a position. When you are a leader, you have authority; however, your authority is not boundaryless. There are two types of authorities: title-based/position and relationship-based.

Title-based authority

This is the lowest level of leadership. In title-based leadership, people follow you because of your position or title. Your influence comes only from your position. Your influence is based on the rights granted by the position and title. Actually, at this level, you are not truly a leader but a boss. You rely on the policies and rules of the organization to get things done. I call it dry leadership. People that follow you will only do what is required of them. This is too limiting because at this level people will only do what is inspected, not what is expected. Your people do not have the motivation to go beyond the call of duty. Bosses and title-based leaders do not motivate or encourage, but demand and command. Such leaders never appreciate one's efforts, no matter how hard you try. These are hard to please leaders.

Everyone who does more than the bare minimum attributes their motivation to great leadership. It is imperative to understand that titles don't make leaders. Margaret Thatcher once said: "Being a leader is like being a lady. If you have to remind people you are, you aren't."

John Quincy Adams said: "If your actions inspire others to dream more, learn more, do more, and become more, you are a leader."

I have nothing against titles per se, but they are often misunderstood and abused. Title-based leaders think they are strong leaders when they are bossy. There is a difference between being bossy and being a strong leader. Bossy leaders misunderstand the nature and purpose of their formal authority. Authoritarian leaders are so task-oriented that they put the work ahead of the human aspects of people. Great leaders are able to strike a balance between being task-oriented and people-oriented. Some leaders discover later that authority is not always effective for influencing people and getting the results that they need.

Linda Hill and Lowell Kent Lineback in their book, *Being the Boss*, indicate that leaders should not rely on the title that comes with a position, or being a boss to get the results they need. Leaders should lead by communicating clearly what they want people to do instead of being bossy.

When you lead by position, you will always feel a need to keep reminding people of your position because you attach your value and self-worth to your position. I know of a pastor who refused to honor a speaking engagement invitation to a conference simply because the invitation letter did not address him with his right title. When leadership is done right, the leader, the church, the organization, and the community benefit. When we do the right things in life, no matter how long it takes, ultimately the right results will come.

Unfortunately, some people find their value in positions; they feel validated by positions. The problem with that is that such a person will not be able to serve outside a position. You should understand that true leadership is when you help people even without a position.

Relationship-based authority

In my doctoral thesis research, I found that relationships are key factors that determine people's level of satisfaction and commitment to any organization.

The best way to lead and develop other people is through relationship building. Relationship-oriented leaders focus on supporting, motivating, and developing individuals in their teams. Leaders are more influential when they build healthy relationships. People are more comfortable and productive when they work with a relationship-based leader than a bossy authoritarian leader.

There is nothing wrong with connecting with your people at a personal level. You may sometimes feel uncomfortable with small personal office talk, but those talks help your people feel comfortable relating to you. You should give people an opportunity to open up and share about their lives and families. People want to work with a real, human, and emotionally connected leader.

A relationship-based leadership style encourages good teamwork and collaboration by fostering positive relationships and good communication. A relationship-driven leader empowers others, and he considers empathy essential to creating strong and productive teams. People want a personal, human, and emotional connection. You have to convince them without any shadow of a doubt that you care about them as individuals, not just as a group. People feel more needed when they are valued, and that could even be a bigger motivation to some of them than just giving them a dry impersonal financial incentive like a raise or bonuses.

Paul took time to build a great relationship with Timothy. Moses had a healthy relationship with his brother Aaron for more than 40 years. A leader may be able to provide shared vision and supervision; however, he must develop a relationship with the people that he inspires. Some leaders hardly think about building relationships with the people they work with. People do not care about your position or how much you know until they know how much you care about them. When a new manager or director joins an organization, the question that his team members are always concerned about even before they meet him is how he handles personal relations with his teams, not how much he will earn or his title.

You don't only want people to be compliant, but you want them to relate. Great leaders win the commitment of their people by winning over their heads and hearts. Every individual in an organization possesses knowledge, skills, and new ideas of potential value. No leader could possibly possess the knowledge, experience, and wisdom needed to make every decision. The organization does not benefit from any team member's full potential if he is not given the space to exercise his gift, skills, and talents. People only commit to an organization that shows that it cares about them.

Successful leaders build relationships and inspire people to become more than they ever imagined. These leaders help people achieve more than they ever thought they could. People trust you more when you have built a good relationship with them. To be effective, leaders need the trust of their teams. They should create and build strong relationships with their team first, then influence them towards a common vision. Relationship building is more important than titles. Successful leadership is based on influence.

The output you get out of any relationship can never be greater than your input. If you are not satisfied with the outcome of your relationship, check how much resources, time, thoughts, and energy you put into it.

People respond better and faster to relationships than to authority. They respond better to relationship building than to your title. No one likes being bossed around. When you boss people around, you are setting yourself up for sabotage. My accountant friend once told me that his boss was so bad that on the week that the national office was coming to audit their books, he would fake being sick. He called in sick on Monday morning and left a voicemail to let his boss know that he was not feeling well, and he was taking sick leave possibly for that whole week depending on how he felt. Their office failed the audits because his boss could not explain some of the expenses on their books, and his boss was fired a month later. Had the boss treated his employees well, they would have reciprocated the treatment and sacrifice for him.

When you lead people, do not think that you have all the authority. Your success depends on your support staff and your team members; therefore, you should treat them well. Farmers know very well that if you want fresh milk from a cow, you have to feed it well in green grazing land with fresh water.

Lifelong vs step leadership

Second chair leadership could be a lifelong calling or a step toward a first chair role.

A lifelong second chair leader is a person who may not be the next leader of the church, ministry, or any organization. Joseph is a good example of a lifelong second chair leader. Joseph was never first in any leadership position his whole life. He was not the firstborn in the house. When he was sold to Egypt, he went there as a slave. He served in Potiphar's house, then went to prison. After prison, he became an assistant to Pharoah. He never became a king or first chair leader. When God has called you to serve under your pastor, serve faithfully without the ambition to take over his position. If you are called to be a lifelong second chair leader, you don't have to push or try to take over from your senior leader. Do not try to manipulate or use people to achieve your ambitions and selfish desires.

Timothy and Elisha are a good example of the step toward first chair leadership. They were being prepared and groomed to take over the ministry. Not all assistant leadership positions lead to first chair leadership. If you stay humble in the sight of the Lord, at the right time He will lift you up. You won't have to push it.

Chapter 9
Submission

And further, submit to one another out of reverence for Christ.
(Ephesians 5:21 NLT)

Submission is one of the most forgotten subjects in churches today. Many people do not see its value and importance. There is a scarcity of preaching on submission and obedience.

The word submission is a conjunction of two words: sub and mission. Sub means under, beneath, or below. Examples of such words are subordinate, subdivision, subway, subcommittee, submarine, subsoil, and substation. It could also mean secondary or next, lower than or inferior to. Submission is an essential attitude if you want to be a successful leader. Submission only happens when a person repeatedly chooses to follow. We all have our mission in life. When you submit, you choose to put your mission under the mission of your leader, your church, or your organization. You choose to make your mission secondary or inferior for the sake of the success of the organization. Once we understand this principle, a lot of infighting in the church will be eliminated.

Bishop Tony Dunn always says, "There is no submission until there is disagreement." True submission is only displayed when your leader or manager takes a decision that may not be your preference. Disagreements cannot be avoided; as long as you work or live with people, you will have some disagreements because you do not all think the same way. If two people think alike, then one of them is not necessary. Disagreements may occur in the church over ministry methodology or programming priorities. It is at that point where submission could be exercised. As long as you are both on the same page, there is no need for submission. It is okay to ask questions for clarification with the purpose of understanding the rationale behind the decision.

How do you respond when your leader does something you disagree with? I do not refer to sinful behavior, but different opinions, preferences, or approaches to resolving an issue.

Take a look at these brief scenarios and reflect on how you would most likely respond. Would you choose to fight, flee, or stay?

Fight, openly disagree, and directly challenge your leader.

Flee, you walk away wounded and offended and feel like giving up.

Stay involved without confrontation, you accept the decision for what it is and stay committed to the ministry.

When your leader goes against your recommendation or preference on a particular decision, or when your leader criticizes a decision you have made or an action you have taken, or when your leader gives someone else a job or responsibility you think you should do or you feel you are more qualified for.

The fight-or-flight response plays a critical role in how human beings deal with stress and insecurity. When we are under threat or feel insecure, our minds quickly rush to either fight or flee.

Confident leaders are relaxed and secure. When you are threatened and fearful, your first response would be to fight or flee. Leaders should be secure. There is power in submission.

Your blessing is in your assignment

Anointing means the grace to do what you were born to do. If you are out of your lane, you may not have the grace and the anointing to serve in that area. If you are graced with the anointing to serve under your leader, stay there and serve faithfully as long as God wants you to stay. When you have been graced to teach, focus on that. Do not try to be a prophet. Stay in your lane, and God will bless you for that.

God expects us to live a life of submission because Christ Himself was humble and submissive. He did not count himself equal with God but humbled Himself to become like us. He took the form of humanity and submitted to the Father in all that He did. God expects us to imitate Christ and humble ourselves just as Christ humbled Himself. When we submit, God promises to exalt us at the right time. The book of James is so clear that we should humble ourselves before the Lord, and He will exalt us.

God resists the proud but gives grace to the humble. No one wants to be resisted by God; all of us need His grace. If you want God to be more gracious to you, you have to be submissive to authority. The purpose of all authority is to protect and bless those who are under its jurisdiction. There is safety in submission and humility; when you submit under authority, the authority becomes your covering and protection. Pride is always followed by a fall because proud people do not submit to authority. Pride, insubordination, rebelliousness, ungovernability, unruliness, defiance, and opposition will expose you to the dangers of life.

The humble and submissive are protected and less likely to fall. Submission results in your protection.

Should we submit to all church leaders?

Submission does not mean blindly following leaders without question. Being submissive does not mean blind loyalty or authoritarianism.

In the church, God has appointed leaders like elders, pastors, and shepherds to oversee the flock. On every level, those in authority are never in absolute authority. Every leader will give an account to God. All leaders, no matter their titles, have to submit to authority. The Bible always talks of having leaders in the church, not one leader. The implication is that in every organization, there should be leaders so that there is accountability. These are leaders who help oversee the church and the senior leader. There should be a plurality of elders over the local church; no leader should be absolutely independent. Absolute independence could mean absolute authority. Only God has absolute authority over the church. Plural leadership safeguards against any abuse of authority.

The Greek words for "obey" and "submit" mean exactly that: to obey and to submit. Obedience implies going along with directions or commands. It is possible for a person to obey without being submissive. A person could obey outwardly, whereas inside he is full of anger, bitterness, and hatred. Just because people are doing what you tell them to do does not always mean they are submissive. Submission is more of a heart issue than a physical issue.

Submission involves a positive attitude and a spirit of cooperation that stems from trust. People submit to their leaders because they trust them. They submit because they are convinced that their leaders have their best interests at heart. It is very important for leaders to create an environment of trust in their organization.

Authoritarian leaders will always impose man-made by-laws and rules that are burdensome to their followers. They always preach that people should submit to them without question. We should remember that pastors are neither infallible nor perfect. You should only submit to your pastors as they also submit to Christ, the head of the church.

The church should submit to godly church leaders. You should only submit to a leader when he teaches God's truth, especially on the essential doctrines and commands of the faith. Anyone who teaches against the Bible is not worth your submission. Matthew Henry in his commentary says that: "Christians must submit to be instructed by their ministers, and not think themselves too wise, too good, or too great, to learn from them; and, when they find that ministerial instructions are agreeable to the written word, they must obey them. Ultimately pastoral ministry centers on Christ and His Message, not on the pastor and his role as messenger. And so to obey and submit to our pastors is a call to esteem, respect, and obey the Word of God. This is why it can be said that 'an elder, leader, or Christian with no Bible is an elder, leader, or Christian with no authority.'"

The pastor's authority is not intrinsic but derivative; believers are commanded to submit only insofar as they are being exhorted to believe and apply scriptural truth. God gave us an excellent example of mutual submission: The Trinity submits to one another. God the Son submits to God the Father, and God the Holy Spirit submits to God the Son, and moreover, even God the Father submits to His Word. God will never violate His own Word.

Chapter 10
Move from Dependency to Interdependency

As iron sharpens iron, so a friend sharpens a friend. (Proverbs 27:17 NLT)

Dependency

Dependency simply means reliance on the functionality provided by some other, external component. A dependent person is like a newly born baby who depends on his mother for everything. He cannot feed himself, he cannot bathe himself, and he can't even speak for himself. In ministry, dependent people cannot do anything for themselves. They depend on someone to pray for them, to read the Bible, and interpret for them. Someone has to keep reminding them to go to church on Sunday or Wednesday Bible study. Dependent people cannot initiate anything. Dependent people rely on what others think; they get their validation from what other people say or how they perceive them. These people have a wheelbarrow mentality. A wheelbarrow will stay where you stopped pushing it until someone comes and moves it.

I used to have a manager who was great at pushing you away from being overly dependent on him. Every time you took a matter or a question to him for guidance, he would lead you to determine the solution yourself. He was a master at asking,

"What do you think?" when in fact you were the one that approached him for help in the first place. He was trying to change our mindset so that we would not be too dependent on him for our performance. Dependency mentality or dependency syndrome makes people expect continued assistance. This undermines initiative at individual or community levels—dependent people never develop.

There is nothing wrong with asking for guidance and direction; however, as a leader, you must know where to draw the line. Try to find a solution for your challenges first before you bring the report to your pastor that you could not do it and you expect him to give you a solution. Let him know of all the other alternative efforts that you tried until you ran out of ideas and options.

God does not want us to be too dependent on other people for our spiritual growth. Spiritual growth is our personal responsibility; we cannot blame another person for our spiritual growth.

Independency

An independent person is free from the influence or control of other people. An example of independence is someone who lives on their own and supports themselves. In most cases independence leads to selfishness because such a person does not care about other people and what they are going through; it is all about him. As the baby grows and becomes a toddler, he reaches a stage where it is all about him. He cannot share his toys with others. As long as he is satisfied, he is okay. This is not what God wants us to do. We have to work with other people in ministry.

Interdependency

Interdependency is the third level of growth. This is mutual dependence, connection, or correlation. At this level, an adult realizes that there is no such thing as self-made success. All of them were helped by someone or some people to be where they are. Mature people understand that we all depend on other people, and in turn, they depend on us. While you want other people to be your resource, you also should become a resource to them and others.

Interdependence is a paradigm of "we," not "I." It's about multiple people being mutually dependent on one another. All the second chair leaders that we discussed were interdependent; they worked together as one team. There was Paul and Timothy, Elijah and Elisha, Moses and Aaron, and Joseph worked well with Pharoah. They understood that there is no "I" in "TEAM." God wants us to move from dependency to interdependence. You can be one team, but you cannot be a team of one. Great leaders have moved beyond the realm of the individual and speak to the dynamics of team, church, organization, community, and society.

As a leader, you have to focus on interpersonal relationships. The more healthy relationships you have, the more resources you will have, and the more effective you will become in ministry. Life is, by nature, highly interdependent. To try to achieve maximum effectiveness through independence is like trying to play tennis alone with a golf club.

Interdependence is the ability to create mutual connections with other fellows, leaders, and ministers who are heading in the same direction as you. Interdependent leaders are sound at managing relationships upward, downward, and laterally.

Dependent people need others to get what they want. Independent people can get what they want through their own effort. Interdependent people combine their own efforts with the efforts of others to achieve their greatest success. Interdependence is a choice that dependent and independent people can make. You choose to invest in building healthy relationships.

Interdependent people take care of their own needs while at the same time caring about others' needs instead of pleasing or ignoring others.

Interdependence leads to unity; the different teams and ministries in the church will start working with one another. The praise team knows that they need the ushers, the evangelism team needs the finance team, the Bible study team needs the prayer team, the Sunday school needs the youth ministry team. We are all interconnected and need each other; there should be no teams that work in silos. There should be no independent team in ministry; the independent spirit will most likely lead to divisions. Teamwork is when we make the team work.

Chapter 11
Teamwork Makes the Team Work

*The human body has many parts, but the many parts make up
one whole body. (1 Corinthians 12:12 NLT)*

A team is not just a group of people who work at the same time in the same place. A team is a group of very different individuals who share a commitment to working together to help the organization achieve its goals and vision. Steve Jobs said great things in business are never done by one person, they're done by a team of people. You can be one team, but you cannot be a team of one. Purpose to work with others for the success of the church. Second chair leaders do their best to build united teams at all costs. If we could not care who gets the credit, we could be more united, effective, productive, and achieve more in life and any organization that we work with.

Teamwork produces dreamwork, and great leaders create an environment for all their people to shine. Successful leaders encourage and develop their people into working as one team to get results in everything they do. The principle is that when you maintain unity, it will lead to teamwork, and in turn, teamwork leads to church growth. It is very difficult to work together when there is no team spirit. The success of your ministry depends largely on developing a strong united team with a deep sense of team spirit. Many churches fail to grow because their team members do not function as a team but as individuals.

A team spirit is never accidental; it is always intentional. A team is formed when people are dedicated to working as one no matter the obstacles and their different personalities. Team members have to put their personal preferences aside and focus on the task at hand. Teamwork is built on a compelling purpose, common vision, clear communication, and a set of commonly held values. If any of these three is not part of the team, it is almost impossible to build a strong team.

Leadership works best when there is collaboration and unity. Paul gave a very simple analogy of how the human body has many parts, but all function as one body. Teamwork is when we have many members and yet one body, one purpose, one vision, and one direction. I have never seen an eye refusing to go where the body wants to go. We have to work together if we want to achieve a particular goal. Team members must learn to be collaborative toward a particular purpose. The main and common focus should be the kingdom of God.

John Maxwell says, "Working together precedes winning together." Not only is he correct, but this also stands as a fundamental truth to the establishment of significant teams. You cannot achieve anything together if you are not working as a team. Team members bring their talents and gifts together and work like a symphony. Synergy is when the cooperation of two or more people or organizations produces a combined effect greater than the sum of their separate effects. That is the power of teamwork.

Collaboration means much more than just working together; it means working together in a synergistic, aggressive, and deliberate manner. You cannot be united by accident. You have to decide to be united. Unity is purposeful. In order to be collaborative, you must have the right perception and attitude.

LEADING FROM THE SECOND CHAIR

Teamwork is essential to the growth and life of the church. No one can do everything by himself. A leader of any organization or church should not try to do all the ministry work in the church by himself. There are things that only he can do; however, there are a lot of things that can be done by other leaders and members. Remember, God spoke to Ezekiel only about prophesying to the dead bones; He did not give Ezekiel all the work. God does not give the work to one person but gives the work of ministry to the entire body. There are some skills and talents that you may not have as a leader. You should give other people the opportunity to exercise their gifts in the church.

Jesus also displayed the power of teamwork in the feeding of the five thousand. Jesus didn't hand out the fish and bread individually to each of the five thousand people. He preferred to share the responsibilities with His disciples. He asked the disciples to tell the people to sit down in groups. Once the people were in groups, He then gave the food to the disciples, and they, in turn, gave the fish and bread to the group leaders. This process shows effective administrative teamwork. Trying to do everything by yourself is not an effective method of leadership.

God did not call you to be a "Lone Ranger" minister; He has called you to be in relational ministry. Christianity is not a religion, but a relationship between man and God, and everything works well when there is a good healthy relationship. God's people should focus on working together for the building up of God's kingdom here on earth.

No matter how skilled the football player is, no player has ever won a game by himself. We all need each other; we need to work as a team. Michael Jordan, the famous basketball player for the Chicago Bulls, knew that, though great, he could not win by himself.

A perfect example of teamwork and how it can help is when Jethro, the father-in-law of Moses, gave him advice on how to lead effectively as a team, not as an individual. Moses wanted all the Israelites who had challenges and issues to come directly to him for help. He would become their counselor, social worker, judge, spiritual leader, and guide. His father-in-law told him that this would not work because at the end of the day, he was tired and ineffective.

Although Moses was an anointed leader, his administrative skills were lacking and would possibly lead him to an early death. His leadership style was not sustainable. We don't know whether Moses was so concerned with the control that he wanted to handle all the cases by himself, or if he did not do self-introspection to think of a more workable, practical system.

Let us see his first statement when he explained his system to Jethro. Moses was really concerned about control and power. This is the kind of attitude that is killing our churches today. The leader feels needed, and he attaches his value to that mindset.

"Moses replied, 'Because the people come to me to get a ruling from God. 16 When a dispute arises, they come to me, and I am the one who settles the case between the quarreling parties. I inform the people of God's decrees and give them His instructions.'" (Exodus 18:15-16)

Check how many times Moses referred to himself in those two verses—more than five times. Let's go back and read the two verses again. He wanted to show or prove to Jethro how much the people depended on him. The first response Jethro gave in verse 17 was "This is not good." When God gave Adam his wife,

He said, "It is not good for him to be alone." He needed a teammate. Thank God that Moses took the advice and implemented it.

Moses had to learn the art of delegation quickly. Jethro proposed a judicial system, which was totally different from the primitive practice of one-man adjudication. He proposed that Moses should recruit good people that he would train and prepare as judges. He would set up a system of courts for different social units, and then a "high court" over which Moses would preside. This kind of system would involve more leaders but save Moses from burnout, and most importantly, it would help the community live in peace and harmony with fewer conflicts and more stability.

In most cases, domineering people have a problem with trusting others. They feel like they are the only ones who can do it right. Most of them have poor reflective and common-sense administrative skills. You have to check yourself as a leader and know what your strengths and weaknesses are so others can help you close the deficit gap. Leadership is not a one-man show. In a symphony, you cannot play all the instruments alone. You cannot be a worship leader, singer, preacher, usher, parking lot attendant, guitar player, drum player, and Sunday school teacher at the same time.

Domineering leaders burn out quickly because they want to control everything. This kind of leadership is hurting and killing a lot of organizations and ministries today.

It is not good to be a leader who is not a team player; you will ultimately become ineffective. If you want to maximize your potential, learn to work with others. Your level of collaboration reveals your heart; you must have the right attitude. There is no collaboration in selfishness. Only teamwork makes the team work.

Chapter 12
Manage the Contentment-Dreaming Tension

For everything there is a season, a time for every activity under heaven. (Ecclesiastes 3:1 NLT)

I cannot stress enough the beauty and satisfaction that come with being content with where you are. Discontented people are easy to identify. They are always complaining, grumpy, and negative about everything. People who are content do not always complain; they tend to have a more positive attitude. A positive attitude will always lead to more opportunities and better relationships.

To be content, a person should first be content with who he is and what he has in his personal life. People's behavior is a true reflection of what is inside their hearts. Jesus put it clearly when He said that what defiles a person is what comes out of his inner being. He also emphasized that out of the abundance of the heart, the mouth speaks. We can only give what we have. A person who is full of joy will be joyful, a person who is full of love will love others, and a person who is full of hatred will hate people. A person who is full of friendliness inside will be friendly outside. People will always treat you as a reflection of what is actually going on in their hearts.

The question that most people have is, is it not a contradiction to be content while you have a bigger vision or ministry that God wants you to fulfill? Doesn't that seem to indicate that one is not content with his life? I believe that not at all. It simply means that one is content with his life, with what he has, and with who he is. Being content means the person accepts that he will always enjoy challenges and the journey of life but is still moving toward a particular goal.

Desires and wants are never meant to be satisfied. Human desires are like seawater: The more you drink, the thirstier you become. The reason we will never be satisfied by desires is that we look to fill the void with possessions or money, but we only end up wanting more. Sometimes we try to fill it with wrong and irrelevant things. All the things that we try to fill our lives with are not necessarily bad things; however, once they become our end goals and our reason for living, we become more discontented because they were never meant to fulfill us. Unfortunately, we get disappointed and get emptier and more depressed than when we started. Remember there will always be someone in a worse situation than yours. The only place that we can really find true fulfillment and contentment is in Christ. A leader who lacks confidence will not lead well.

Second chair leaders are often faced with the challenge of finding contentment in where they are while dreaming of the future. Leaders have dreams and visions of where they want to go in life. Dreams have a place in life, but they should never replace the reality of the present. Life is a series of seasons, and so is leadership. Life is a series of phases, and God may fulfill your dreams and vision in phases. Your current season and phase are not your end. Where you are currently is just a season; at the right time, you will move to the next phase of your life.

Sometimes the tension between dreams and contentment can be pretty severe. As a Christian leader, you have to learn to contain the unending, internal push for a brighter tomorrow. You have to be gratefully content with where you are today. Shy away from the temptation to compare yourself with other people.

There will always be someone with a bigger house, a faster car, bigger ministry than yours. It takes a certain level of maturity to understand that right now you are at the place where God wants you to be. For now, focus on serving the Lord faithfully where you are, and when the right time comes, God will put you in the right place. Where you are right now is also part of the vision that God gave you. You should have a vision and desire to do more for the Lord, ministry, and people, but do not allow things and positions to define you. You are complete in Christ even without a position. It takes maturity to be content and understand that when the season for your next assignment comes, God will open the doors for you. You do not have to push or try to convince someone. Once the Lord opens the door for you, nobody can close it.

True contentment is not something that we find in things, people or circumstances, but can only be discovered in our personal convictions. Real contentment will only come from accepting Christ and having faith that in Him we are complete. Contentment is not simply about settling for what we have but trusting in what God has said. Positions and titles do not make us. We need to accept that Christ is sufficient, and His promises are enough.

You can only be content with where you are if you humble yourself and ask God to help you understand that all situations, including your current one, are temporary. Nothing is permanent in this world.

Chapter 13
Leave a Legacy

Good people leave an inheritance to their grandchildren. (Proverbs 13:22 NLT)

I have no greater joy than to hear that my children are walking in the truth. (3 John 1:4)

One of the most important aspects of leaders is what happens after they are gone. I have seen big ministries and churches fall apart after the leader died. Some of them can't even be traced a few years later. I have also seen some ministries and churches that continued to grow and touch many lives even after the leader has died. All the leaders that I know, or that I have worked with, have one thing in common: They want to leave a legacy. Focus on building a church, ministry, or organization that will outlive you; refuse to let the church die with you.

Brooks and Stark define legacy as what makes a person unforgettable. Your legacy has nothing to do with your position; it is about who you are as a person. You are the one who leaves a positive legacy, not your position. You can create an inspiring leadership legacy no matter your position in any organization or church.

Legacy could be any belief systems, materials, or behaviors that the current generation passes on to the next one. By legacy, we are not only talking about the transfer of money, wealth, or physical assets but values as well. Money is good and needed; however, it is not a lasting legacy. True wealth is found in our values and belief systems. Our spiritual inheritance has more impact than money. Actually, it could help sustain the financial and material heritage beyond our physical presence. Studies show that the financial inheritance families receive, whether large or small, is gone in an average of 17 months. David Green, the founder of Hobby Lobby, in his book, *Giving it All Away,* stated that only about 30 percent of family businesses survive into the next generation. The other 70 percent do not survive and successfully transfer to the next generation. John Maxwell in his book, *The 21 Irrefutable Laws of Leadership,* wrote, "A legacy is created only when a person puts his organization into the position to do great things without him." Leaders should focus on leaving a lasting legacy.

People observe how their predecessors behave and imitate them. As a leader, you should always plan to leave a lasting legacy for your ministry, church, and family. Legacy is when a leader uses his ministry to change lives. We have to make the necessary changes so that we can pass the right behavior, influence, and culture on to the next generation. We cannot give them what we do not have. We cannot teach them what we do not know. We have to pass our spiritual and financial heritage to the next generation. Spiritual legacy includes teaching them to pray, read the word, and serve God. Paul set an excellent example of a good legacy when he transferred all that he knew to Timothy. Today we are still enjoying his legacy. Leaders should focus on the long-term effects of their decisions, for the decisions we make today will affect many generations to come.

A pastor's legacy could be determined by the leadership he puts in place and the people that he disciples. It is so important to spend time and focus on building the emotional and spiritual health of the church. Spiritually healthy Christians are rooted in

Christ. It is more important to build a spiritually healthy church than a big, crowded church. Only spiritual legacy will last; crowds that are not spiritually mature will not last for long because they are focusing on meeting their personal selfish needs and what they can get out of you. The church should not be centered around a person but Christ because He is the same yesterday, today, and forever. Christ will never change. Leaders should pray for the spiritual growth of their members, especially in the area of prayer and the reading of God's word on their own.

Leaders should be role models of faithful stewardship, both financially and spiritually. Your life should serve as an example to the church because people watch how you live and what you do. Invest in the lives of your members. Be more than a preacher—be a teacher. Your ministry will have a lasting impact on people's lives when they realize that you care about them and see value in them.

As long as you influence change in the lives of people around you, you are a leader. You have to leave others with a lasting legacy. You don't want your efforts, ministry, and projects to have been in vain. You cannot build a lasting legacy with crowds. Jesus knew from the beginning that for the ministry to last, He had to focus on the small group of 12, not the 5000. He spent a lot of time training them and explaining parables and concepts to them such that by the time He left, He knew that He was leaving a solid group that would depend on their training and the power of the Holy Spirit for their ministry success.

Identify a small group that you will mentor and disciple one on one. You cannot disciple crowds; you will have a greater impact when you focus on a smaller group. The key to effective discipleship is focusing on impacting the lives that will impact other lives. The ministry is multiplied when we reach other people and train them to reach others. One of the characteristics of great leaders is that they take it as their responsibility to raise up and equip others who are called into ministry. They take the time to teach them to be good stewards of their calling. Biblical faithfulness is foundational for Christian leaders who leave legacies.

Any leader who wants to leave a lasting legacy will need to change their perspective on what successful leadership really is. Such leaders are secure, confident, and humble. Secure and confident leaders, especially among believers, know that their security and their confidence come from the Lord. Confidence simply means holding and trust that God will fulfill what He promised us. Leaders who leave a legacy use their power and their authority to serve other people.

Whether you are aware or not, you are leaving a legacy; the only question is what kind of legacy are you leaving? Kouzes and Pisner say, "The legacy you leave is the life you live."

The question that you should always ask yourself is, "Am I in this world to do something or I am here just for something to do?" To be here for something to do means you are ready to do anything that comes your way. If you are in this world to do something in particular, then what is it that you should do or focus on? This is a question of your purpose for living. This is not a mathematical question, so there is no single correct answer. We all have our own assignments as individuals.

You are born for a purpose. Just because you do not know your purpose does not mean you do not have a purpose. You cannot afford to simply leave your legacy to chance. You have to consciously draft and craft your own legacy. You have to start focusing and doing things that matter the most to you. You should also understand that not everyone will value what matters to you; therefore, do not get upset when some people do not support what you do. As you focus on doing what is right and what matters to you, sometimes you will have to make unpopular choices and decisions regarding your careers, school, lifestyle, associations, church, and ministry. It is important to make the right choices in life because every choice that you make will automatically become part of your legacy. As you live your daily life, you are creating a legacy. Your legacy is a sum total of the difference you would have made in the lives of people.

Success in leadership is not only measured in numbers but by what you do to change the lives of other people. Authentic leadership focuses on serving others. All great leaders focus on providing a good service to the people that they lead. Whatever difference you make in people's lives will become your legacy.

Chapter 14

See Your Senior Leader as a Gift from God

And He gave some as apostles, and some as prophets, and some as evangelists, and some as pastors and teachers, 12 for the equipping of the saints for the work of service, to the building up of the body of Christ. (Ephesians 4:11-12)

A little farther up the shore he saw two other brothers, James and John, sitting in a boat with their father, Zebedee, repairing their nets. And he called them to come, too. (Matthew 4:21)

All Scripture is God-breathed and is useful for teaching, rebuking, correcting and training in righteousness, so the servant of God may be thoroughly equipped for every good work. (2 Timothy 3:16-17)

Now may the God of peace, who through the blood of the eternal covenant brought back from the dead our Lord Jesus, that great Shepherd of the sheep, equip you with everything good for doing His will, and may He work in us what is pleasing to Him, through Jesus Christ, to whom be glory for ever and ever. Amen. (Hebrews 13:20-21)

Your leader is a gift from God. His main assignment is to equip or prepare the church for the work of ministry. The Greek word for repair or equip in all these verses is *katartizo*, which means to mend and prepare for purpose. It could also mean to renew, to complete or perfect or furnish with intellectual or emotional resources. When the first readers of these passages saw the word *katartizo* in everyday use, they understood it very well. The word was commonly used in finishing or completing something and making it ready for use, like a fishing net, a boat, a house etc. The purpose of being equipped was that the equipment would be fully prepared or restored and readied for service. This is exactly what God wants to do in our lives.

Your pastor is there to prepare you and help you deal with your spiritual and even emotional challenges so that you are ready for the ministry. Emotional healing is very important if you want to do ministry work.

In Matthew 4:21, the two brothers James and John were mending or preparing their nets so that the following day when they started their shift, the nets would be ready for service. In case the nets were broken, they would mend them, clean them, and put them together again. Paul used the same word in the Ephesians to remind us that we are saved for service in the kingdom of God. However, before we can serve, we need to be mended and prepared first. As a leader, you should allow God to use His tools to mend your broken heart.

You cannot walk properly with a broken leg. You cannot do ministry with a broken heart. Broken people bleed, and if you are not healed, unfortunately, you will bleed on innocent people. If you are not emotionally healed, it will be difficult to connect with your people and build genuine relationships. God gave us the leaders like apostles, prophets, evangelists, pastors, and teachers to prepare us for the work of ministry.

All of us have a purpose. You were born for a purpose, and the church acts as a base from which you are launched to execute your purpose. Your leader is given to you to prepare you for the fulfillment of your purpose; he prepares you to discover and fulfill your purpose. Every time you see your leader, recognize him as a gift. When we receive gifts, we appreciate them, we love them, and use them for our convenience. Their purpose is to equip the saints. Leaders are there for the mending (repairing) of the saints. We thank God for giving us such a great gift.

Yes, that pastor is to feed his flock. He is to tell us what the Bible says and help us to grow as God's sheep. And as you can see from this verse, the gift is given from God's own heart. It is God's desire for the pastor to help us. It's God's will for the under-shepherd to watch over us. That matter of the pastor is God's will altogether. Now I'll show you some of the jobs the Bible has given to the pastor, then apply it to your daily lives and how it affects you.

The pastor is to use the word of God to help perfect us. That is why God gave us the Bible and a preacher to preach it to us. The perfecting is done by fully furnishing us. When we get saved, it's like getting our house cleaned. God saved you from the lifestyle you were in. God made you a new creature. So you have an empty house. The pastor is to give us godly things to fill the house up to make it worthy of Jesus living in your heart.

A gift is something we say thank you for, is it not? But when was the last time you thanked God for your pastor? A gift is something we cherish (at least I do), but do we cherish our pastors?

The point is this: your pastor is a gift straight from heaven. His words and encouragement are meant for building us up as Christians. Yet how often do we roll our eyes or ignore him or sleep straight through a sermon he prayed and asked God for direction?

On the flip side, when a church is selecting its leadership, do you see how important prayer is? If every pastor is handpicked by Christ and gifted by Christ alone, then we'd best be seeking God's will in the matter. A lack of prayer, moving ahead of God, will only get us into trouble.

Because make no mistake, it's God who gives the church a pastor, a teacher who is willing to speak the truth in love and take on the very serious job of leading God's people. So instead of grumbling, instead of complaining, instead of sleeping, let's thank the Lord for His gifts. Let's thank the Lord for our pastors, who are a gift from Christ Jesus Himself—who is absolute, perfect, and one hundred percent the best gift-giver I know.

Contemplate and evaluate: Are you thankful and supportive of your church leadership? I would suggest that you honor your pastor with encouragement and support as you feel God directs you.

Chapter 15
How to Leave Your Church

*Don't use foul or abusive language. Let everything you say be good
and helpful, so that your words will be an encouragement
to those who hear them. (Ephesians 4:29 NLT)*

When it is time for you to leave the church, ministry, or
organization, do your best to leave peacefully. When you feel like
it is time for you to leave, do it in a Christian way rather than
always complaining. There is nothing wrong with leaving
voluntarily if you reach an impasse; however, you need to check
your heart and make sure you are not leaving out of anger but in
a peaceful way.

Good leaders leave their organization in better shape than
they found it. They leave the organization in a better financial
position than when they came. Do not create chaos when you
leave. It is always good to leave but still keep healthy
relationships. Life is so unpredictable; you never know who you
will need or whose reference you will need in the future. Your
reputation is your most valuable asset; you should jealously guard
it.

Do not speak badly about your previous leader, pastor, or
supervisor. The way you speak about them reflects on your
character and reveals your heart. Remember, when someone
speaks badly about another person in your presence, when you
leave you are most likely the next item on their agenda.

Let no corrupt words or communication come out of your mouth when you leave. Do not intentionally destroy your path, connections, reputation, or opportunities with the church that you are leaving. Even if the separation was not on good terms, do not burn your bridges on your way out, because you never know who you will meet again. We live in such a small world, so no matter how tempted you might be, do your best to keep the lines of communications open.

There's no reason to make enemies when you part ways with your senior pastor; you would also like them to speak well of you. Your reputation precedes you everywhere you go. A good reputation will ultimately work to your advantage.

Important things to remember when you leave

Tell your senior leader or pastor first

Be transparent with your leader. Once you have decided to leave, your pastor should be the first one to know. Your pastor should not hear the news from anyone else. Let the leader decide if he will announce the news in a team meeting or email or if you will be responsible for telling key people in the organization. You should establish an up-front culture in your organization to keep the rumor mill at bay. When you are honest and straightforward about your plans, you own the narrative. The more transparent you are, the more likely you are to preserve and build on the relationships you already have.

Your former ministry partners and coworkers are a valuable part of your network. You need to keep those relationships healthy and intact.

Don't gossip

A gossip betrays confidence, but a trustworthy person keeps a secret. (Proverbs 11:13)

A perverse person stirs up conflict, and gossip separates close friends. (Proverbs 16:28)

With their mouths the godless destroy their neighbors, but through knowledge the righteous escape. (Proverbs 11:9)

Remember that there are no secrets and no off-the-record conversations in the workplace.

No matter how much offended you could be, avoid spreading rumors or gossip about your leader. You don't have to destroy other people's reputations to be a better person. Never make the mistake of giving different reasons for your departure to different groups; it will come back and damage your reputation. There should only be one story, told one way, and if you stick to it, nobody can ever say they heard anything different.

When you start gossiping about your pastor, or any person who has wronged you, you are fueling the flames. Avoid any form of gossip at all costs. There are lots of friendships that have been broken because of gossip. When you hear that a person you trusted has been speaking badly about you, trust will be broken. Gossip does not help with reconciliation, but only brings more divisions. Some people feel like they become better by destroying other people's reputations or by speaking badly about them. The way you speak about other people is a true reflection of your heart, for out of the abundance of the heart the mouth speaks.

Regardless of your reasons for quitting, you have one final responsibility to your church or organization. Do not give them reasons to regret your association, membership, or affiliation with them. Make sure you don't leave your pastor in a pickle; do your best to collaborate with him.

Discuss with him how you should tie up loose ends. You want your pastor or senior leader to feel nothing but positive about your integrity even in your leaving. There is always a great likelihood that your paths will cross again. It is always exciting to reunite later in life when you parted ways in a healthy way.

Express gratitude

Sometimes it is not easy to leave the people that you have been working with for a long time. You need to adopt an appreciative mindset about the position and people you're leaving behind. Even in the worst situations, there are parts that you enjoy and colleagues you like working with. You need to be grateful for the things that went well. It would be nice to send out some modest farewell gifts or thoughtful notes to your pastor, leader, direct supervisor, mentors, and others that you served with. Leaving a good and positive impression will work to your advantage. You could leave notes like "I am grateful to have worked with such a wonderful group of people" or "I appreciate the time you spent mentoring me and helping me to grow my skills and in ministry."

If you are dealing with a leader who takes your departure personally, just trust God that He will help him understand that there is a season for everything under the sun. Sometimes it is not productive to try to change his mind.

Talk freely with the other members and colleagues

You could be tempted to be brutally honest when you leave and want to give detailed information on everything that's wrong with the church or ministry. This is not the right time to give the feedback or advice you wish you had given while you were part of the organization. At this point, your feedback is not going to change the church or organization. Avoid venting temptation and emotional conversations. In case you have some differences with your pastor, handle them in a godly and healthy manner.

PART D
How to Lead from the Second Chair

And you should imitate me, just as I imitate Christ. (1 Corinthians 11:1 NLT)

People follow their leaders, and as a leader, you should be able to speak like Paul and encourage your followers to imitate and follow your example. Being a leader worth following will among other things involve the following:

- Pray for your leaders and their family
- Focus on making your pastor's vision a reality
- Be a source of encouragement and appreciate your leader
- Be faithful, available, and teachable
- Keep a positive spirit
- Receive admonishing with grace
- Communicate with your pastor
- Be an exemplary leader

Chapter 16
Pray for your leaders and their families

I urge you, first of all, to pray for all people. Ask God to help them; intercede on their behalf, and give thanks for them. 2 Pray this way for kings and all who are in authority so that we can live peaceful and quiet lives marked by godliness and dignity. 3 This is good and pleases God our Savior. (1 Timothy 2:1)

D.L. Moody said, "Every movement of God can be traced back to a kneeling figure."

Never undermine the power of prayer; your pastor needs your prayers. No matter what you do to show support for your pastor, nothing can be compared to prayer. The best gift you can offer to your pastor is to pray for him. People can offer their hands until they are all worn out with serving or give money for great projects and causes in the church or do all kinds of amazing things together as a church, but none of these good deeds will ever be a substitute for the covering and lifting power of prayer.

To show real support for your pastor, commit to pray effectively for him and his family daily. Just imagine how encouraged your pastor would feel to know that you and your family are praying for them daily. Their hearts will be lifted if they know that they can share a need or a concern with you and your family and you will take it to the Lord on their behalf.

If you were not aware, a lot of pastors and their families feel very alone even in the midst of their churches. Pastors experience times when the challenges seem impossible. Most pastors do not have close friends in the congregation with whom they can share their challenges and burdens. Remember, the pastor's family is just like yours; they have challenges, struggles, and problems too. Pastors are not immune or superbeings; they are susceptible to the same weaknesses as any other Christian. Be that reliable friend who is always available when your pastor needs a shoulder to cry on. Be that friend whom the pastor can be vulnerable with and can literally cry in your presence without a sense of being judged. Your pastor needs you to commit to fervent, continuous prayer so that the enemy won't have the opportunity to do damage to him, his family, and the church. Be the number one intercessor for your pastor. Pastors need your prayers for many reasons, but mainly because they are always the object of the flaming arrows of the evil one, the world is eager to run them over at any opportunity, and the media is waiting to celebrate their fall.

Pastors are experiencing so much pressure, opposition, and difficulty within and without, they always need you to pray for them. The shepherd needs the prayers of the sheep as much as the sheep need his prayers. Your pastor's ministry will only be as effective as the prayer that fuels it. Here are some specific ways that your family can pray for your pastors and their families:

- That pastors and leaders can diligently stay the course
- For unity in your church
- For their courage and strength
- For their wisdom to increase
- That they can fulfill the mandates of Scripture and minister out of a humble spirit

- That they will be equipped to minister from the power of the Holy Spirit
- For the families of your pastors
- That they will be people of prayer and the word
- For their spiritual protection against the schemes of the devil
- That their focus will increase

Recruit as many people as you can to pray regularly for your pastors and their families. It is important that you cover them in prayer seven days a week. Ask the Lord to show you more things you can do to show your love and appreciation to your pastor.

Chapter 17

Focus on Making Your Pastor's Vision a Reality

Where there is no vision, the people perish: but he that keepeth the law, happy is he. (Proverbs 29:18 KJV)

Your pastor's vision should always be a priority. Avoid the temptation to push your own vision or agenda inside the main vision. There is no church or organization that can survive with two visions; two visions always lead to di-vision. God gave your pastor a vision. Please work with him in making it a reality. God put you in that position to help your pastor, not to compete with or criticize him.

Every sermon has a purpose and objective. Be the first one to show support to your pastor or leader by cooperating with him and be the doer of God's word. Be the first one to tithe or give when it is time to do so—lead by example. When there is fundraising for courses like missions, building funds, or any other project, be the first one to support your pastor. Do your best to focus on helping your pastor's vision succeed.

Vision simply means to see the final product even before you start. A vision gives a sense of direction. There is a difference between vision and sight; that is why even a blind person can be a leader. A blind person may not have sight, but a vision for the organization or family. Vision serves as the propeller for any organization to keep moving. You cannot afford to lead an organization without a vision.

When the vision is clear and people know where they are going, they can easily set aside many smaller issues and focus on the bigger picture and the future that is worth their sacrifice. A vision sustains people in hard and troubled times; it always reminds them of the purpose behind your ministry. In organizations and churches where the vision is clear, there are fewer squabbles and arguments. If you as a leader are always putting out fires, do some self-introspection and make sure that your members and the leadership understand your vision. Spend some time at least once a year or as often as possible and share your vision with your church. Keep on reminding your teams and members of your vision so that you all have the same point of focus. I have found that people do not support you; they support your vision. The clearer the vision, the more support you will have from your people. A clear vision will unite your people and give them hope. A vision sustains people in hard and troubled times; it always reminds them of the purpose behind your ministry.

If you have a project that resonates with or appeals to their conscience, people will support you wholeheartedly financially, physically, and otherwise. Establishing a clear, compelling vision will guide leaders' efforts and keep them moving.

Chapter 18

Be a Source of Encouragement and Appreciate Your Leader

As iron sharpens iron, so a friend sharpens a friend. (Proverbs 27:17 NLT)

To appreciate means to give deserved recognition for the work that someone does. It also means to respect and have positive regard for them. Your pastor needs your encouragement. It is important to understand your pastor's love language and serve him in a way that would make him feel encouraged and appreciated. Garry Chapman in his New York Times best-selling book, *The Five Love Languages,* discusses the five love languages that each one of us speaks. Your love language is your interpretation and understanding of what it means to be loved. I believe we can use the same principles to show our love and support for our pastors and senior leaders. Here are the five love languages that he discusses:

Words of Affirmation

Use words to affirm and compliment people who feel loved or show their love through verbal praise, compliments, and expressions of love. It means saying the assumed and unspoken about someone. Saying words of appreciation means the world to the person. Expressing appreciation and gratitude to the person in words means that you love them.

Acts of Service

For these people, actions speak louder than words, and true love is shown by doing things for them. Be alert for any opportunity that arises for you to serve and make use of it. Be available to help your leader when he needs your thoughts, effort, or even physical energy. Sometimes he may need someone to help with packing chairs, teach a Sunday school class, clean the church, or help with ushering. Any act of service speaks volumes.

Receiving Gifts

Some people like things or gifts to feel appreciated. They love receiving presents ranging from small tokens to surprise deliveries. They appreciate it if you buy them something they've been wanting for a while, send them a surprise package, or sign them up for a class they've been wanting to take.

Quality Time

This means giving someone your undivided attention. Spend time together in a relaxed atmosphere. Be emotionally present with him and give him your full attention. Listen to him when he shares his heart and concerns about the ministry or his personal life. Your pastor may need your attention especially when there is a conflict or experiencing some emotional pain. To quality time people, listening is a true gift of love. This could be your opportunity to show them compassion and support.

Physical Touch

Appropriate touch like shaking hands, pats on the back, or a hug will mean a lot to a person whose love language is physical touch.

According to Chapman, words of affirmation are the most

common primary love language for a lot of people. Do not miss an opportunity to let your pastor know how much you appreciate him. The most common of the five love languages are:

- Words of affirmation: 23%
- Quality time: 20%
- Acts of service: 20%
- Physical touch: 19%
- Receiving gifts: 18%

Learning your pastor's love language will help create a stronger bond in your relationship. You may discover your pastor's love language by watching their behavior. What makes them light up? What language do they most readily give to others? Or by simply asking them.

Do everything you can to pump life into your pastor's soul, build him up, encourage him, lift him up, inspire him, and bless him in Christ. Communicate with him and let him know how much his service means to you. Show love and kindness, be a conduit of grace, hope, and love to build him up. Be a source of motivation. Be considerate and help him get spiritual, emotional, mental, and physical rejuvenation.

Chapter 19
God Loves FAT People
Be Faithful, Available, and Teachable

Be a Faithful Servant Leader

If you are faithful in little things, you will be faithful in large ones. But if you are dishonest in little things, you won't be honest with greater responsibilities. (Luke 16:10 NLT)

Faithfulness is the core of integrity, sincerity, and dependability. Faithfulness is the glue that holds the ministry together. No ministry, relationship, or church can survive without faithful leadership; even society cannot function normally without it. Be steadfast and constant in your service and ministry. Consistency and reliability is the only way one can build trust. God blesses and increases faithfulness in His ministry.

There is a difference between being involved and being committed. Being involved is when you do something out of convenience, whereas being committed means you give out everything you have. A very good illustration is in a bacon and egg sandwich. Two animals have been involved for you to enjoy the bacon and egg. The chicken laid the egg, and continued to live, whereas the pig had to die for you to enjoy the sandwich. By the time you eat the sandwich, the pig is dead, whereas there is a possibility that the chicken is still alive. A chicken was just involved, whereas a pig was committed. Are you involved or you are committed to the ministry? Be committed to the ministry; do not be the reason your pastor spends sleepless and restless nights. Be available to help him, give him all the support that he needs.

It is worth mentioning that we are not saved by our good works, but by God's grace. There is no amount of serving in the church, ministry, or community that can save anybody. Ephesians 2:9 is very clear that we are not saved by our good works because God does not want anyone to boast about it. We are saved by God's grace and through faith in Him alone. Though we are not saved by our good works, God expects us to repent and start doing good works after we are saved. Verse 10 emphasizes that we are not saved by good works, but we are saved for good works.

When we serve people, we are changing lives. True leadership is when you focus on helping and changing the lives of the people that you are leading. As a leader, you should support them and help them grow in their relationship with God and people, academic goals, parenting, careers, financial management, and many other aspects of their lives.

Leadership is influential, and true influence involves building trust and a relationship, getting people to align their views and values with your own for achieving a particular goal. You can't influence a person until he perceives you as someone who is there to serve him. You have to help him bring real change in his life. People will come to your church when they know they will be served, cared for, and their lives will be impacted in a positive way.

In the '70s, Robert Greenleaf at Fuller Theological Seminary in Pasadena introduced the concept of Servant Leadership. I believe the first servant leader was Jesus Christ himself. Jesus kept emphasizing that *"He who is greatest among you shall be your servant."* (Matthew 23:11)

As a servant leader, you are a servant first before you are called a leader. Larry C. Spears, former president of the Robert K. Greenleaf Center for Servant Leadership in Pasadena, lists the following 10 most important characteristics as the pillars of servant leaders: stewardship, commitment to the growth of people, listening, empathy, healing, awareness, unselfishness, conceptualization, foresight, and community building.

Servant leaders serve the people they lead, not vice versa. A servant leader focuses primarily on the growth and well-being of people and their communities while traditional leadership generally involves the accumulation and exercise of power by one at the top of the pyramid. Jesus was the most perfect servant leader that ever lived.

15 As evening approached, the disciples came to him and said, "This is a remote place, and it's already getting late. Send the crowds away, so they can go to the villages and buy themselves some food." 16 Jesus replied, "They do not need to go away. You give them something to eat." 17 "We have here only five loaves of bread and two fish," they answered. 18 "Bring them here to me," he said. 19 And he directed the people to sit down on the grass. Taking the five loaves and the two fish and looking up to heaven, he gave thanks and broke the loaves. Then he gave them to the disciples, and the disciples gave them to the people. 20 They all ate and were satisfied, and the disciples picked up twelve basketfuls of broken pieces that were left over. 21 The

number of those who ate was about five thousand men,
besides women and children. (Matthew 14:15-21 NIV)

Every miracle that Jesus performed had a purpose and a lesson. In this miracle where Jesus fed the 5000, there are a few lessons of true servant leadership that we can learn.

As leaders, we are leading people with needs, as in Verse 15: "Send the crowds away, so they can go to the villages and buy themselves some food." The followers of Jesus needed food at that point. Servant leaders understand that people have spiritual needs, health needs, emotional needs, relationship needs, and many more. Every person that you lead has a need. As a servant leader, identify the needs of your followers and help them find a solution. Some people may need salvation or physical help, some need emotional healing, whereas some just need to be encouraged.

We should point people to Christ, who can meet their needs, as in Verse 15: "The disciples came to him and said, 'This is a remote place, and it's already getting late.'" The number one characteristic of a cult is when the leader is the main person and point of focus. In Christianity, our focus is Christ, the author and the finisher of our faith. Forward the needs of your followers to Jesus through prayer. A good servant leader is a good intercessor. You do not have all the answers for people's needs; only God can meet their needs. Don't discount the impact of prayer in any situation.

God expects you as a leader to give. Verse 16: "Jesus replied, 'They do not need to go away. You give them something to eat.'" Be willing to give your resources, donate money, and be hospitable. Sometimes you may be required to sacrifice and give your time to your senior leader, ministry, and the people that you lead. The multiplication of food took place as they distributed it in the hands of the recipients. God is Jehovah Jireh; He will always provide for His people. Trust God for multiplication in your resources. My mentor, Dr. Moses Shipalana, used to advise me that if I take care of God's business, God will take care of my business. No amount of giving and sacrifice for the kingdom is in vain.

Don't be extravagant; be responsible. Verse 20: "They all ate and were satisfied, and the disciples picked up twelve basketfuls of broken pieces that were left over." You should have clear financial accountability systems. Be a good steward of people's finances. Remember, every penny counts. Spend money only on what the ministry needs. God provides more leftovers when we are faithful in the little that we get. He is a God of more than enough. Once people spot or sense any form of financial maladministration, they will stop giving. Be transparent with people's finances. Do not give people any reason to doubt you.

Learn to delegate others. Verse 18: "Then he gave them to the disciples, and the disciples gave them to the people." Don't try to be a superstar and do everything by yourself. Teach others, encourage them to take classes on budgeting, writing, taking minutes, keeping records. If there is a need to improve the skills of your leadership, encourage them and send them to school or institutions where they can acquire those skills that they need. You may send them to computer school, leadership seminars and conferences, colleges, or universities. People perform better when they are equipped. Train and teach others to do what you are doing. Paul had Timothy, Moses had Joshua, and Elijah had Elisha. Who are you training to do what you are doing?

Count the cost—numbers matter. Verse 21: "The number of

those who ate was about five thousand men, besides women and children." Numbers are important; they should become your friends. Numbers don't lie, and in this passage alone we find the following numbers: 5000 men, 2 fishes, 5 loaves, 12 apostles, and twelve baskets. Know your numbers to be a good leader. You can't manage what you can't count. Don't be allergic to numbers. The Bible is full of numbers from Genesis to Revelation, and actually, there is even a book that is dedicated to "Numbers" because numbers matter to God. Some leaders are allergic to numbers, but numbers will work to your advantage. You have to know how many members you have, how many were saved in your crusade or revival, how much is your monthly income. Count the cost and know how much it would cost to build the next auditorium or children's building. Budgeting, numbers, and accountability are unavoidable in leadership. The wise king does not go to war without checking if he has enough soldiers to fight his enemies.

When Jesus fed 5000 men, He displayed true Servant Leadership in practice. This is the example that He has set for every leader to follow.

Be available

To be available means that you are accessible when you are needed. When your pastor needs you, you should be available. Are you available to God whenever, wherever, and however He leads and directs you?

Samuel is a prophet who played a key role in the transition from the period of the biblical judges to the institution of a kingdom under King Saul. He helped again in the transition from Saul to King David. *"The Lord called Samuel and he answered, 'Here am I.'"* (1 Samuel 3:4 NKJV) Samuel was mightily used by God because he made himself available. When God calls us to do something for Him, do we obey or do we feign ignorance? Are we available or do we give excuses?

Be available to help other members of your church or organization when they need you. It's your responsibility as a leader to help your members see their potential, use their God-given gifts, and grow in their leadership. Your goal isn't recruiting; it's starting a relationship. Get to know members of your church. Ask great questions and listen to their answers. Learn about their families, jobs, passions, and hobbies. Then, help them understand the roles your church has that fit their passions and giftings. Some leaders automatically discount attendees in their church because they think they won't be interested in serving or don't have the time. Ask them anyway. Many people would love to serve and are just waiting for you to ask. It is important to appreciate your volunteers, whether it's face-to-face, in a text message, on social media, or in a handwritten note. Thank your volunteer team.

Be teachable

Nobody knows everything in life. We must have hunger and thirst for knowledge and be willing to learn and grow. It is so encouraging to work with someone who is open and willing to be taught. You can tell if someone is teachable by how he responds to things you try to impart to him. One of the biggest disappointments is when you try to work with someone who thinks he has it all figured out. People who have a teachable spirit admit that they do not know everything. They do their best to search for information from Scriptures, people, or other sources like books. They always have a sense of curiosity; they want to learn and grow. They are also willing to transform their life based on the new information that they acquire. Some people just have a lot of information with no transformation. Leaders should allow the word of God to change them. A learning leader is a growing leader. Great leaders are great readers. If you do not read you will mislead people.

Growing leaders are faithful, available, and teachable. May God help us to be FAT, stay faithful to Him and His Word, and give us the courage to be available and teachable.

Chapter 20
Keep a Positive Spirit

And now, dear brothers and sisters, one final thing. Fix your thoughts on what is true, and honorable, and right, and pure, and lovely, and admirable. Think about things that are excellent and worthy of praise. (Philippians 4:8 NLT)

Be a compliment, not a competitor to your leader. Inject a positive influence in the church. The most difficult people to work with in any organization are people without a vision and those with a hidden agenda. These people will always be negative about anything their leader does; they will complain about everything from his sermon all the way to the color of the carpet. Do not be a constant complainer. Negative people try to influence others to be like them: the spirit of disobedience is contagious. In life, we will probably attract people of the same kind like us, and we love to be surrounded by them. Misery loves company, so we know that miserable people will always get attracted to each other.

It is dangerous to be the one who is always complaining and unappreciative. In Numbers 16:32, the Bible speaks of the Israelites who were murmuring, and God finally opened the earth to swallow them alive. What your mind dwells on matters to God. If your mind is centered on good thoughts, you will have a positive spirit; however, if you dwell on negative thoughts, you will have a negative spirit.

A positive spirit is contagious. You will influence a lot of people by being supportive and positive. People always want to be a part of something meaningful and inspiring.

As people encounter you, they detect your attitude. Barnabas stood out in the young church because he had the spirit of encouragement. Furthermore, he looked for the good in people. When others were afraid to trust Saul, he urged them to give the former enemy of the church a chance. Later, John Mark deserted a missionary journey. Barnabas opened a way for the young man to rejoin the mission work again. Faced with the Jerusalem Christians' concerns about embracing gentiles, Barnabas encouraged their acceptance. In every way, he was the opposite of the self-promoting ways of Diotrephes. I pray we have more people with the positive spirit of Barnabas in the church.

Paul begins by telling us that the best way to develop a positive spirit is by having a positive attitude toward our spiritual leaders, those who work hard among us, those who sacrifice their time and energy to serve the Lord. We're to respect, honor, and encourage them in what they do for God.

Thinking positively, speaking positively, and acting positively will be a great help to the ministry and to your leader. The book of Joshua encourages us to meditate on the word of God day and night. By meditating on the word, we can identify three clear models for developing a positive attitude the way God intends. We will think positively because our thoughts are significant in shaping our attitude to life. Speak positively because there is power in the tongue. We need to keep God's word in our mouths by making positive affirmations and confessions of faith that are biblically sound. When we make this a habit, we will be surprised at how they can positively change our attitude toward life.

We will then act positively. Our lives and behaviors are based on our belief systems. It is important for us not to be just hearers of the word but to go a step further and do the things we have heard. Faith without works is dead; our lives should be a true reflection of our faith.

Chapter 21
Communicate with Your Pastor

Fools find no pleasure in understanding but delight in airing their own opinions. (Proverbs 18:2 NLT)

Communication is not a monologue but dialogue. Communication involves the coding and decoding of a message. Effective communication involves conveying a message to another person, but for it to be effective, the recipient must understand the message and respond. When communicating, do your best to listen more than you speak. Improving your communication skills will lead to better relationships and ministry growth. Relationship growth is directly proportional to communication skills. The more and better you communicate the more your relationships will grow. Jesus constantly communicated with His disciples. He would always say, "He who has ears let him hear." He wanted to make sure that His disciples mastered listening skills, for without that skill they would not understand Him. Here are a few things you need to remember when communicating with your pastor or other people.

Communicate in their language

It is always advisable to understand your pastor's personality and preferences regarding his communication style. Ask him how he prefers to be informed or kept in the loop of what is going on in your committee or ministry. You may schedule weekly or monthly meetings, depending on his schedule. The more you meet, the more in sync you will be in ministry. Some pastors prefer phone calls, and some are okay with texting, whereas some prefer in-person meetings. If your pastor prefers a phone call, then pick up the phone and call. The way you communicate with him could be one way to honor your pastor. Exchange your views and advice with him as often as possible. You will understand his vision better when you communicate. Vision is not taught but caught. Share helpful ideas for the benefit of the church or ministry. Be open and communicate with your pastor about your weakness or the weakness of your ministry so he can help you whenever you need it. Ask him or communicate with him about his vision and mission for the church.

Keep your pastor informed

Your pastor needs to know what is happening in the church. He needs to know even those things you think he does not care about, especially in a situation where something has gone wrong.

Anything that happens in the ministry that you oversee, your pastor should hear it from you first as his closest leader. Get as much information as you can, and report to him immediately. In case you make a mistake, be the first one to let him know. Nobody else should disclose to the pastor what you should have disclosed to him. He is the leader of the congregation, so he should have an overview of the ins and outs of his church.

Let your pastor know that you understand that he is a human being. Sometimes he may make mistakes. If your pastor knows that you will support him despite his flaws, he will definitely be assured that he can count on you. Never keep secrets from your pastor. If you hear something that could be negative for the church or harm the ministry, let the pastor know so he can take care of it.

Never say negative things about your pastor

If you have an issue with your pastor, talk with him directly about it. Most pastors appreciate it if you communicate with them directly rather than gossiping about them. In case you do not feel comfortable, it is always advisable to take someone with you. Gossiping about your pastor is not helping you resolve the situation. Do not make the mistake of thinking that you have all the information. No matter how much you know about a situation, you may not have all the facts. Communication is the only way to get all the information that you need. In reality, we rely on a biased set of cognitive processes to arrive at a given conclusion or belief. This natural tendency to cherry-pick and twist the facts to fit with our existing beliefs is known as motivated reasoning—and we all do it.

In life, we make decisions based on the information that we have. You make better judgments and decisions when you have all the information. Never assume you are always right and everyone else is wrong. If your pastor is involved in something sinful, immoral, or illegal, follow your church's policies and procedures so you can involve the relevant people or authorities. In all your efforts, do your best to move toward reconciliation and restoration through biblical standards.

Chapter 22
Receive Admonitions with Grace

To learn, you must love discipline; it is stupid to hate correction.
(Proverbs 12:1 NLT)

The next day, Moses took his seat to hear the people's disputes against each other. They waited before him from morning till evening. 14 When Moses' father-in-law saw all that Moses was doing for the people, he asked, "What are you really accomplishing here? Why are you trying to do all this alone while everyone stands around you from morning till evening?" 15 Moses replied, "Because the people come to me to get a ruling from God. 16 When a dispute arises, they come to me, and I am the one who settles the case between the quarreling parties. I inform the people of God's decrees and give them his instructions." 17 "This is not good!" Moses' father-in-law exclaimed. (Exodus 18:13-17)

There will come a time when you need to be corrected. We all make mistakes, and you should be willing and humble enough to be corrected. When your pastor tries to correct you, take it with a good and positive spirit. He wants to see you win and succeed. Your pastor is not your enemy; he is not waiting for your fall or failure. He wants to correct you because he loves you. The problem is in most cases, we struggle so much with pride it is difficult to receive corrections graciously. People accept corrections with mistrust and suspicion.

Exodus 18 helps us understand that God is so kind, He had Jethro and Moses give us an example of what humble correction looks like on both sides. Moses took advice from Jethro, his father-in-law who was not even a Jew, but a Midianite. Most probably he didn't even believe in Jehovah, the God of Israel. Moses was humble enough to receive corrections from Jethro. God can use anyone in our lives to help us or correct us. We should approach every situation with an open mind and willingness to be corrected. We can learn something from anyone we come into contact with in life.

Most people find it so difficult to receive corrections because it is rarely delivered in a pleasing manner or context. The other reason could be that the person who delivers the corrections could be flawed, maybe even worse than them. Sometimes people do not receive corrections because of insecurity, low self-esteem, and self-deception. It is rare to hear the following words when a person is corrected, "Thank you very much. I needed that." Instead, people get angry, offended, defensive, and start to attack the messenger.

It is advisable to resist being defensive and argumentative; it is not a wise thing to do. You may find that there is some truth in what the other person is saying. Even a broken clock is right twice a day. We all have some blinds spots in our lives. Not every correction may be completely true or necessary; however, almost all have a kernel of truth. It is advisable to press the pause button and learn something from the conversation. Wise people allow corrections in order to grow.

This could also be applicable in your personal relationships. Maybe the reason you're struggling with your relationship could be that you do not listen when your spouse tries to advise you. As a leader, you have to lead even in correction because it is not easy to lead others to places that you have not gone. If you can't be corrected without being offended, you will never grow in life. Great and exemplary leaders receive corrections with wisdom and humility, setting a powerful example for their followers.

Chapter 23
Be an Exemplary Leader

Don't let anyone think less of you because you are young. Be an example to all believers in what you say, in the way you live, in your love, your faith, and your purity. (1 Timothy 4:12 NLT)

A leader's character must be exemplary, otherwise, his credibility is undermined, and he will lose respect from those who are supposed to follow him. Paul encourages Timothy to be an exemplary leader in the way he conducts himself and relates to others. Your followers are interested in going where you have gone before. Take them where you have been and let them know what took you there. If there is a project that the pastor wants the whole church to be involved in, be the first one to do it. People learn by your example. Let them see you do it; let them see you support your pastor. Your actions speak volumes to the members. You have to lead by example even in prayer meetings, building campaigns, evangelistic campaigns, or any program that needs people's participation. Even if you may not be scheduled on the program, just be there and be supportive; your presence is a motivation to others. It is called the ministry of presence.

Share Christ and your church with others

"Nazareth! Can anything good come from there?" Nathanael asked. "Come and see," said Philip. (John 1:46)

Our number one mandate as Christians is to share the good news with unbelievers. The final instruction that Jesus gave us was the great commission. Sharing the gospel should be the main focus for the church and all Christians. Sharing the gospel is the only activity that has eternal value. Sometimes we just need to invite people to church with the hope that they will hear the gospel and accept Christ as their personal Lord and savior. You do not have to be a theologian to share the gospel. You could speak like the Samaritan woman who believed in Jesus and quickly went to invite others. She did not have any theological training; her only message was "Come and see." John 4:29

Philip could not convince Nathaniel that Jesus was the Messiah; his only words of invitation were, "Come and see." Jesus did not send us to argue with people until they repent, but He said we should go and preach the gospel. The Holy Spirit is the only one who is responsible for convicting people to come to Christ. Let people know about your church and share your testimony on how God has used your church to change your life, your family, and other people. Be an ambassador for Christ and his church.

Encourage other church members to invite their friends, colleagues, and families to your church. Personal invitations are more effective than social media, advertising, and other forms of marketing combined. Pray for the people that you invite to church; there is power in prayer. A church that has a culture of inviting is more likely to grow than a quiet church. People will typically feel much more comfortable attending a new church when they already know someone there.

Chapter 24

How to Increase Your Value in Your Organization

For God so loved the world, that he gave his only begotten Son, that whosoever believeth in him should not perish, but have everlasting life. (John 3:16 KJV)

What is man that You are mindful of him, And the son of man that You visit him? (Psalm 8:4)

I would like to clarify that before God we all have equal value; God loves all of us the same. John 3:16 is very clear that we are all loved by God, no matter our background or what we have been through in life. You have great value before God and know that He will always love you. The Psalmist is also very clear that God always thinks about us, we all have value before God. As human beings, we cannot increase or decrease our value before God. The value that we are referring to in this book is people's perspective and demand for your services, help, and personality. We all have equal value before God. However, people do not have equal demand for us. Some people will have a greater demand for you than others. People's perspective of you depends on how helpful you are in helping their organizations, families, ministries, and their lives grow to the next level. You have greater value to the people who need you than to those who do not. People will value you for your leadership skills, knowledge, accomplishments, personality, and for how you help them grow when they are around you. Hopefully, this helps clarify the purpose of the chapter on how to increase your value.

The first question could be: What does it mean to be a valuable person, leader, pastor, teacher, minister, husband, wife, child, or employee? Merriam-Webster defines being valuable as having desirable or esteemed characteristics or qualities. This means being of great use or service in the community, ministry, or any organization. In life, you can make yourself more valuable to people, church, or any organization that you're attached to if you consciously make some adjustments and relevant changes. In any organization or corporate world, you can only move up the corporate ladder by making yourself more valuable. You can also strengthen your relationships and make them last longer by making yourself more valuable and necessary.

You can add value to the value chain or systems of the organization or institution that you are attached to right now by the type of contribution you make to its growth. You should constantly ask yourself one question, "What value am I adding to this family, relationship, committee, church, or organization?" Successful people make themselves valuable and indispensable in their organizations by making themselves relevant and necessary. In this section, we focus on how you can make yourself valuable through education and personal development. Having a job that you love can be quite fulfilling; however, if you want to move up in your career, leadership, or gain greater job security until nobody wants to get rid of you, you have to make yourself invaluable.

See Value in Education

Then the king told Ashpenaz, his head ruler, to bring in some of the sons of Israel, both those of the king's family and of the important leaders. They were to be young men, perfect in body, good-looking, with wisdom, understanding,

much learning, and able to serve in the king's house. The
king told Ashpenaz to teach them the writings and
language of the Babylonians. And the king gave them a
share of his best food and wine every day. They were to be
taught for three years, and after that they were to serve
the king. (Daniel 1:3-5 NLV)

Daniel and his friends Shadrach, Meshach, and Abednego were slaves in Babylon. King Nebuchadnezzar wanted them to come and serve in his palace. These young people were naturally gifted; however, the king wanted to make sure that before they could come and serve, they had to go to school first. Just like any degree takes an average of three years, the king wanted them to learn for three years. The reason Jesus spent three years with his disciples is that on average it takes about three years to train a person in a particular discipline. Universities and colleges also call these areas of learning *disciplines.* After three years in the university discipline/faculty or program, you would be trained as a teacher, engineer, pharmacist, agriculturist, or any profession of your choice. If three students graduate from the same high school could attend the same university, but choose different careers, like, pharmacy, education, or agriculture, they will all go through different academic programs. After three years of being in different disciplines, they will graduate with different perspectives of life and nature. When they look at the same plant, they do not all see the same thing. A teacher may see a teaching aid, the pharmacist may see medication, and the agriculturist may see its fruit. The purpose of discipleship is to help a person see life differently.

King Nebuchadnezzar knew and understood the value of education. For a person to be of value in any organization, education plays a pivotal role. We need educated people in our governments, ministries, churches, organizations, and communities. If you want to be able to bring real value to the ministry, do not undermine the value of education. Before they could serve in the palace, King Nebuchadnezzar wanted them to get some education first.

Paul put it very clearly in 2 Timothy 2:15 (KJV): *"Study to shew thyself approved unto God, a workman that needeth not to be ashamed, rightly dividing the word of truth."* He emphasized the need for Timothy to study as he got into the ministry. Yes, Daniel, Shadrack, Meshack, Abednego, and Timothy were anointed, gifted, and very smart, but still needed education. God appointed them for specific duties and responsibilities in ministry and in government; however, they still needed education so they could learn about leadership, ministry, government systems, and protocols.

They had to sharpen their axes and skills in order to be more effective. By studying and learning, they were increasing their value. Just because we are saved and filled with the Holy Spirit does not automatically make us valuable in the education, political, market, technological, and financial systems that govern our world. No matter how smart, gifted, or skilled you are, someone will always be better, more skilled, more knowledgeable, and smarter than you. Make a decision to learn from those who know more than you do. God will always bring people around you, and some will be more intelligent and well-informed than you are. You have to make a conscious effort to surround yourself with people who know more than you do. In actual fact, if you are the smartest person in the room, don't be proud; you are in the wrong room. You should go to the room with people who are more knowledgeable, smarter, educated, and wiser than you. There are so many benefits to surrounding yourself with people who are smarter than you. Allow other people to challenge your mindset, your belief systems, and your intelligence in a positive way. We all have the capacity to learn and grow. If you are committed to paying the necessary price, you can learn anything that you want to achieve in life. Christians should not be allergic to education; as Christians, we should have hunger and desire for knowledge. *"An intelligent heart acquires knowledge, and the ear of the wise seeks knowledge."* (Proverbs 18:15 ESV)

When you are educated, you have more opportunities in life. On average, you earn more money than an uneducated person. Most organizations would prefer you to an uneducated person, and your quality of life will comparatively be much better than an uneducated person. Educated people have more and better opportunities than uneducated people. In most industries, educated people hold higher positions than uneducated people. Educated people make more informed decisions than uneducated people. In order to make yourself more valuable, continually improve your skills through education. Your education is your responsibility; nobody else is responsible for your development. Education can be formal or informal; you can learn from the classroom or from life outside the classroom. It's important to maintain a desire to learn and hone your craft, whether it's by acquiring new skills, seeking continuing education, attending seminars and conferences, or even just reading books, magazines, and journals that are related to your subject. Besides having valuable skills and expertise, it's important to behave and hold an attitude that makes you a key ingredient of the organization, ministry, or company's success.

Never stop learning

*My people are destroyed for lack of knowledge; because you have
rejected knowledge, I reject you from being a priest to me.
And since you have forgotten the law of your God, I also
will forget your children. (Hosea 4:6 ESV)*

Many dreams, visions, relationships, or even organizations
have died because of ignorance or lack of knowledge. In life, it is
very difficult to progress or make sound decisions without
relevant information and knowledge. Our decisions are as good
and helpful as the amount of knowledge we possess about any
situation. The more information we have about a situation, the
better and more informed decisions we make. Presidents want to
make sure they have daily briefings with their ministers or heads
of departments so they will always have fresh information. This
helps them make sound, synergized, and well-synthesized
decisions. God says a lack of knowledge will result in a lack of
progress in life. If you think education is expensive, try ignorance.
In most cases, we pay for our ignorance in life.

One morning my neighbor could not start her car. She tried
everything that she knew, but the car would not start. She then
decided to have a mechanic in our neighborhood come and fix
the car. The mechanic came and opened the hood, touched a few
wires, then asked the lady to start the car. Surely the car started,
then he charged her $100. She was surprised that he charged her
so much for a problem that did not even take three minutes to
resolve. She was so worried the whole week. One day she decided
to call him and ask him what was the problem with the car. He
frankly told her that the battery terminals were loose, so he
tightened them. As she was dealing with the shock, he told her,
"I charged you only $5 for tightening the loose terminals;
however, I charged you $95 for knowing where the problem

was." In life, we pay a lot for ignorance. If we had knowledge, we would not pay for a lot of things and services that we pay for every day. Ignorance or lack of knowledge is more expensive than education. Just imagine how much you would have saved if you learned and knew how to do a lot of things by yourself.

The only reason we pay the mechanics or electricians to fix our cars or electrical systems is that we do not know how to fix them. Once we know how to fix the problem or a situation, we do not have to pay someone to do it for us. All problems are a knowledge gap problem. When you have a problem you always say, 'I don't know what to do.'. Once you know what to do, then your problem is solved. Education helps us become more knowledgeable about a particular subject. Remember, you will never be educated enough.

When I learned how to use Excel spreadsheets way back in the late '90s when Microsoft had just introduced their Windows Operating System, one of my instructors said something that I will never forget. He said, "Abraham, everything you do in Excel or any computer program, there is always a better and faster way of doing it." That stayed with me until today. I use the same principle in my way of thinking and life. There is always a better way of doing anything in life; my responsibility is to keep finding that better way through education and development.

"Every day they continued to meet together in the temple courts. They broke bread in their homes and ate together with glad and sincere hearts." (Acts 2:46 NIV)

The early church understood the value of continuously meeting, growing, and learning. They continuously met and learned from each other because they understood that in order to be of value in the church, they had to grow in the knowledge of the word of God. In the manufacturing industry, it is called a CIP or CI (continual improvement process). This is an ongoing effort to improve products, services, or processes. These efforts can seek "incremental" improvement over time or "breakthrough" improvement all at once. We should all check the areas of our lives and organizations where we need CIP. Whatever you are doing in life, you have not reached the ceiling or pinnacle of knowledge; there is always room for improvement. There is always a better way of doing it. I once interviewed a candidate who applied for a position in one of the organizations I was attached to. I remember asking him about his skill set in a particular program that we were using. I asked him "On a scale of 1 to 10, how would you rank your skills level?" This new, fresh candidate, who had just completed his master's degree in business, said, "Nine."

That response cost him a job. When I evaluated his response, it gave me the impression that he felt like he did not have anything new to learn. Considering that he did not even have any previous practical work experience in this field, how could he rate himself at that level? A lot of people miss the opportunity to grow because they feel like they have arrived. They convince themselves that they know everything. In life, people have a tendency to hold on to belief systems and convictions that work against their progress. The Bible is so clear about continuous reading and learning from the word of God. *"This Book of the Law shall not depart from your mouth, but you shall meditate in it day and night, that you may observe to do according to all that is written in it. For then you will make your way prosperous, and then you will have good success."* (Joshua 1:8 NKJV)

If you want to grow, do not overrate yourself. None of us are educated enough. We should believe in continuous improvement, then we will be effective and valuable in every area of our lives. Continuous growth will help you increase your value.

Stay current with technology and trends

Oxford Languages Dictionary defines technology as science or knowledge put into practical use to solve problems or to invent useful tools. Merriam-Webster defines technology as a manner of accomplishing a task especially using technical processes, methods, or knowledge. Technology is an extension of the human hand. Technology helps us do things faster and even reach places and people we would not reach on our own. It helps make processes run faster. The way things are done today is not the same as it was 20 years ago. Processes and methods change so rapidly that we should make efforts to keep up with the changes. In order to stay relevant and valuable, you have to change with time.

Remember, you may not change the principles, but the methods. As Christians, we should not change the essence of the gospel, but we may change the way we spread it. Paul had to use camels, ships, or walk to different nations in the scorching heat of the Middle East to preach the gospel. They would spend many days, weeks or even months on the sea moving from one country to the next. Today, I can fly to any country in the world within 24 hours because of technology. I usually fly from Los Angeles to Johannesburg in 24 hours. I can drive to cities and villages much faster than Paul did in the first century. Technology and industry trends are constantly changing.

In order to be an invaluable asset to your organization, you have to continually learn new technologies and keep up with the trends. Make a decision that you want to become the go-to person for certain skills in your organization. Your knowledge and skills will make you more valuable than those who refuse to stay up to date. There are some great phone companies like Nokia, Ericsson, and BlackBerry that either refused or were slow to transition and adapt to the smartphone technology. These companies are nowhere to be found now; their names have become insignificant in the cellphone industry. Their technology has become obsolete. Do not be like those companies. Valuable employees do not just do their jobs, but also increase their knowledge and expertise to prepare for future challenges. If your current skills or knowledge is not improving with the current trends in your field, make it a top priority to improve and gain new skills. In today's workplace, hard work and effort are no longer enough to assure success or even to guarantee continued employment. Advances in areas like technology, business, innovations, competitions, and dynamic customer needs have pushed organizations to adapt to the new way of doing things. Accomplishment at work is no longer just about working harder but having a competitive advantage. Competitive advantage refers to factors that allow a company or an individual to produce goods or services better or more cheaply than others in the same industry. It could simply mean working differently and ensuring your continued value. Set goals and be self-disciplined to educate yourself. The key is to stay focused and be deliberate. Increasing your value is a must if you want to be effective and influential in ministry and life in general.

Some suggestions for educating and developing yourself

- Register with a school of ministry, Bible college, university, seminary, or other institution of learning.
- Read for at least half an hour every day.
- Read books and journals that are related to the subject area of your interest.
- Stay current on the news about your subject of interest.
- Teach others about what you have learned.
- Join book clubs.
- Attend conferences and development seminars.
- Sign up for online courses.
- Find mentors for every area of your life.
- Talk to experts and ask questions.
- Read biographies of legends.
- Make Google your best friend.
- Use YouTube as your resource; watch videos that are relevant to your area of interest.
- Attend courses through your current employer.

As Christians, we should discourage ignorance. The reason some people take advantage of some Christians and their finances is that most of them are too lazy to read the Bible and discover the truth for themselves. Personal daily devotions should be a must for every Christian. You will learn more when you spend time with God the Father, the Son, and the Holy Spirit than when you wait for someone to come and predict your future and call it "prophecy." If you're doing the same work, ministry, or leadership in the same way you did two years ago, chances are you're being left behind and irrelevant. Soon you will become insignificant or obsolete. You can increase your value in the organization by growing your knowledge and skills. Your church will benefit more if you make yourself more valuable. Life is like riding a bicycle: The moment you stop pedaling, you lose balance. To stay valuable, you have to keep learning. The more you know, the more valuable you are. By embracing change and learning new things, you will demonstrate a drive for innovation and a model for others in the organization to follow.

"Give instruction to a wise man, and he will be still wiser; teach a righteous man, and he will increase in learning." (Proverbs 9:9 ESV)

You should strive to make the ministry, church, department or organization feel your influence by improving the processes and methods and continuously growing. Every living thing that God has created grows. God put you in that position because He wants you to make a difference in people's lives.

Conclusion

Leading from the second chair means that all of us can be leaders irrespective of our positions. Once you understand that you can serve even without a position, it is so liberating and will minimize the infighting and tensions that exist in most churches. You can lead from the pew, you can lead as an usher, you can lead as a minister, and you can lead as a Sunday school teacher. Once we understand that leadership simply means influence, then we start to understand our role much better. Leadership is not a position or a title, but a function. Anything that you do to help the senior leader is part of leadership. The main goal is to advance the kingdom and the vision of the local congregation. We all have a role to play. Do not wait for a position; as the old song says, "Brighten the corner where you are."

Notes

Begg, A. (1996). Pharaoh's Dream from Series: The Hand of God (Volume 1). Sermon Transcript

Blaiklock, E. M. (1965). The Young Man Mark (9-21).

Brooks, M., Stark, J., & Caverhill, S. (2004). Your Leadership Legacy: The difference you make in people's lives. Berrett-Koehler Publishers.

Green, D. (2017). Giving it All Away... and Getting it All Back Again: The Way of Living Generously. Zondervan.

Hill, L. A., & Lineback, K. (2011). Being the Boss: The 3 imperatives for becoming a great leader. Harvard Business Press.

Kouzes, J. M., & Posner, B. Z. (2006). A Leader's Legacy (Vol. 101). John Wiley & Sons.

Marxsen, W. (1969). Mark the Evangelist. Nashville: Abingdon.

Maxwell, J. C. (1993). Developing the Leader Within You. Harper Collins.

Maxwell, J. C. (2007). The 21 Irrefutable Laws of Leadership: Follow them and people will follow you. HarperCollins Leadership.

Spangler, A., & Tverberg, L. (2018). Sitting at the Feet of Rabbi Jesus: How the Jewishness of Jesus can transform your faith. Zondervan.

Swete, H. B. (2006). The Gospel According to St. Mark. Wipf and Stock Publishers.

Warren, R. (2012). The Purpose Driven Life: What on earth am I here for? Zondervan.

The Author

Dr. Abraham Manase comes from Tzaneen, Limpopo in South Africa. He and his wife, of over 25 years, Mihloti, have been blessed with three children: Nsovo (Grace), Timothy, and Hope. For the past 20 years, they have been living in California, where he serves as an ordained elder at New Day Christian Fellowship under Bishop Tony Dunn. He has been serving in ministry for more than 30 years.

Dr. Manase obtained his B.A. Ed from the University of Limpopo in South Africa, post-graduate studies in business management from the University of South Africa (UNISA), and his MBA from Hope International University, Fullerton, CA. He holds a Doctor of Business Administration degree from Columbia Southern University, Orange Beach, Al. He is also a graduate of Water of Life school of ministry in Fontana. He serves on a number of local and international boards in diverse industries. He traveled extensively throughout the world doing leadership development and training. He ministers internationally through his weekly radio and television ministries. He is currently a professor of business leadership at Myrtle Beach Wesleyan College in Myrtle Beach, SC, and a senior data management analyst for a major organization in Orange, CA. www.drmanase.com.

Made in the USA
Monee, IL
05 August 2023